D0442674

THE USE OF PUBLIC POWER

The Use of
Public Power

ANDREW SHONFIELD

Edited and introduced by
Zuzanna Shonfield

Foreword by Sir John Hicks

Oxford   New York
OXFORD UNIVERSITY PRESS
1982

Oxford University Press
and associate companies in
BEIRUT   BERLIN   IBADAN   MEXICO CITY
LONDON   OXFORD   NEW YORK
GLASGOW   TORONTO   MELBOURNE   WELLINGTON
CAPE TOWN   NAIROBI   DAR ES SALAAM   LUSAKA   ADDIS ABABA
DELHI   BOMBAY   CALCUTTA   MADRAS   KARACHI   LAHORE   DACCA
KUALA LUMPUR   SINGAPORE   HONG KONG   TOKYO

British Library Cataloguing in Publication Data
Shonfield, Andrew
The Use of Public Power.
1. Economic policy   2. Economics—history
—20th Century
1. Title   II. Shonfield, Zuzanna
330.9181'2   HD82
ISBN 0-19-215357-9

Library of Congress Cataloging in Publication Data
Shonfield, Andrew, 1917–1981
The use of public power.
Includes index.
1. Economic history—1945–   .   2. Economic policy.
I. Shonfield, Zuzanna.   II. Title.
HC59.S495   1982   338.9   82-8252
ISBN 0-19-215357-9

Printing: 9 8 7 6 5 4 3 2 1

Printed in the United States of America

Foreword

BY

SIR JOHN HICKS

The Use of Public Power – Andrew Shonfield's own title for the book which was to begin with the chapters which follow – can be recognized as an echo of the subtitle of his earlier book, *Modern Capitalism* (1965). He there spoke of the 'balance of public and private power'; and it may well have been that that was a better description of his subject. For what he meant by 'Modern Capitalism' was the mixed economy, with large public sector and large private sector, which appeared to have become the dominant form of economic organization, in very many countries, at the time when he was writing. It appeared, at that time, to have been an outstanding success. In purely statistical terms the rates of growth which had been achieved in the previous decade (and longer) were quite remarkable, standing out from previous experience. And they had been achieved with very little of the ups-and-downs which, on previous experience, had accompanied growth. The new system was not only remarkably productive; it was also remarkably stable.

What, he asked, were the characteristics which gave it the possibility of this outstanding success? He used his wide knowledge of the institutions and the policies of the countries of Western Europe, in particular, to guide him to an answer. The most explicit answer was handed to him, he found, by the French. For it was in France, more than elsewhere, that the marriage between capitalism and planning had become a doctrine, with a formulated principle, and practice that agreed with that principle as well as could be expected. The principle was one of paternalistic planning: an economy led by bureaucrats, skilled bureaucrats, so skilled that they would really know better than the industrialists and labour leaders with whom they had to deal, so could impose their wills by their superior knowledge. The cruder sorts of compulsion would be unnecessary when persuasion, coupled with powerful inducements kept in reserve, could do all, or almost all, that was required. The moral authority which was required for such a system to succeed was provided, in Shonfield's opinion, by a long tradition of expert bureaucracy, going back to Colbert and Napoleon. (One might ask whether it really was such a continuous tradition: I shall come back to that.)

After France he turned to Germany. In France, doctrine and practice went together; in Germany they were far apart. While the politicians, to the bewilderment of observers, hymned the praises of free enterprise and passive government, direction was in fact provided, in a manner not so very far removed from the French, by a non-governmental bureaucracy, that of the banks. The German orchestra did have a conductor, but he was to be found in the Bundesbank, not in the government. This did not make all that difference.

When he turned to the cases of England and of America, there was indeed more trouble. They did not fit well into the European pattern, and their performance, during the period considered, was distinctly less good. Was one the cause of the other? It was tempting to blame the British for the amateurishness of their civil service, and the Americans for their 'pluralism'; but though there might be something in that, it was not very convincing. Was there not more that was common to the experience of all the countries surveyed than could be explained in terms of 'dirigisme'? Shonfield had an open mind; I think he was aware, when he finished writing that important book, that some of the biggest questions he had been considering still remained open.*

---

* I have been drawing, rather heavily, in the preceding paragraphs on a review of *Modern Capitalism* which I wrote for the *Guardian*. I felt that it was proper to do

So he was to come back to them in a new book, of which the chapters that follow were all he could finish. He now had fifteen more years of experience on which to draw – fully fifteen years, for the events of 1980 are fitted into place, though he survived for less than a month after the end of that year. He even knows about the election of President Reagan, and could guess, quite correctly, what would follow from it. He does not of course know about President Mitterrand; but would he have been surprised?

The performance of all his countries during the latter period, which had now to be taken into account, was much less of a success story than it had been in the earlier. Growth rates, though in most cases they were on average still respectable, were decidedly down; the stability, which had been praised, was largely gone. How much of his old viewpoint, in the light of these misfortunes, would he find it possible to keep?

It is notable that he no longer finds it possible to proceed by countries, treating their experiences rather separately, as he had done in his former book. (He does indeed find it necessary to give special attention to one country, Japan, which he had there put on one side. For Japan, in later days, had been the most faithful to something like the 'dirigisme' of the old sort.) For the rest of his countries, it is the closer association between their economies, which has grown up in these years, that he chiefly emphasizes. Imports and exports, mainly to other members of the group of 'developed' countries, have as a share of total production been markedly rising, to heights which in earlier times would have been thought to be very dangerous (Germany is an outstanding example). International treaties, making for freer trade, facilitated the movement; but (as Shonfield, surely rightly, maintains) they did not cause it. It is both cause and effect of increasing affluence; specialization increases, while the advantage of being able to purchase a wider range of goods than can be produced in one's own country is more highly prized. This is a tide against which it is hard to swim. The Japanese can do it, since they have a traditional way of life which is very different from that of their Western competitors, so that it can only be transformed into something more

so, for I know that Shonfield liked that review and it is no doubt for its sake that I have been asked to write these pages.

'developed' by slow degrees. That is surely beginning to happen. For the present, however, Japan has a natural protection, under the shelter of which economic direction is easier. Those who do not have that protection must expect to find that their planning is continually thwarted by external pressures – the balance of payments problems with which we have become so familiar.

It is easy to understand, in the light of these considerations, how there should be pressures for the renewal of contrived protection; but this, as I read him, Shonfield rejects. This is partly because he thinks it unlikely to be effective, unlikely to be carried so far as to be effective, since the forces that are making for interdependence are so strong. What he would prefer is to work for a better co-ordination between national arrangements. He can point to two examples of such co-ordination. The first, rather successful, was on the occasion of the first oil shock of 1974, when an expansion of credit, internationally, did prevent the developed countries from cutting each others' throats. There was a real danger that each of them, confronted with a balance of payments crisis, would seek to meet it by cutting imports indiscriminately, including imports from each other, while it was a righting of the balance with OPEC, of the developed countries taken together, that was required. The second was the attempt to engineer a recovery in 1977–8, 'loco-motives' and 'convoys', a story which Shonfield finds particularly interesting, though it was a failure. It was cut short by the second oil shock of 1979; he nevertheless holds that it was right to attempt it, and that it should not have been cut short in the way that it was.

The standpoint which he adopts on these matters is consistent with his philosophy; but perhaps he does not quite face up to the extent to which these experiences put his philosophy in danger. The remedial measures that were taken in 1974–5 were accompanied, in nearly all of his countries, by a great inflation of prices; and it is not surprising that the inflation of prices should have been ascribed to the credit expansion. I think he is right in his view that the association, apparently so obvious, is false. If there had been no expansion of _international_ credit, the national inflations, which were essentially cost-inflations, would not have been much, if at all, diminished (there would still have been national monetary expansions to meet the rises in costs); while the real contraction, in output and in employment, would have been much greater. One can go that far with him; but perhaps he gives too little weight to the seriousness of the inflation, a major worry to all the governments. It was not just because they were listening to monetarists that Mrs Thatcher, and then President Reagan, have taken such deflationary measures after the second oil shock. They have had a problem.

One must not give the impression that extension to the problems of the international community is the main thing that is new in these chapters; there are several other strands, one of which, at least, should be noticed. There could well have been some readers of the former book who were surprised that he did not accept that definition of the mixed economy that had become conventional – the 'Welfare State'. An enormous expansion of social expenditure had been a common experience of his countries; of course he knew that, but it can now be seen that he did not want to stress it, for the view which he took of it was rather special. He did not regard it in the way it was so often presented, as being in the interests of 'the poor'; he saw that it was itself another consequence of the increasing affluence. It did not work in the interests of the poorest classes, which have not come so well out of it; for it had been more truly devised in the interests of the 'average man'. That man, the median man on the scale of inequality, was no longer a proletarian; with increasing wealth he had begun to take on middle-class characteristics. He had assets – and liabilities; he had a way of life which he wanted to have preserved. From that much follows, on which Shonfield had good things to say.

Some of the less economic aspects – the political, administrative, and social aspects – of his *Modern Capitalism* had been the subject of a concluding section of that book. I think it is clear that what would have corresponded to that rather brief discussion was intended to be the major part of the later work, as planned. It is greatly to be regretted that we do not have it. How one would have wished (for one thing) to have had his further reflections, informed by new evidence, on the evolution of the bureaucracies. I have said that I doubted whether the force of the (modern) French bureaucracy had much to do with Colbert; I should have liked to ask him if, after all, it was not much more to be attributed to the new blood that came in, after the old people had gone down with Vichy. Bureaucracies must have time to establish themselves; so continual change, on the American model, is ineffective. But they do need renewal, a renewal of freshness, and they cannot at all easily provide that themselves. It is very sad that we cannot ask him these questions, and get the wide-ranging answers he might have given to them, surveying not only his European countries but also Russia and China.

Contents

Introduction

'The mixed economy is everywhere reviled; it is pronounced to be sick and its demise is freely predicted; yet in a large part of the Western world it continues, with apparent vigour, to go about its daily business.'[1]

To explore this seeming paradox has been the object of much of Andrew Shonfield's writing since the late 1950s. By 1980, in the fifteen years since the completion of his *Modern Capitalism*, there had been important changes. The text of the present work was devised partly as a critical analysis of prevailing economic theories, partly as a history of economic practice and its consequences. It was intended to set the scene for a full-scale re-examination of the balance of public and private power after the economic shocks of the 1970s.

The work was interrupted by the author's death in January 1981, shortly after he had checked the definitive draft of Chapters 1 to 3 of this book. Of the remaining topics, several were in first draft

This book is part of a series of publications sponsored by the Economics Department of the European University Institute, Florence. The editor wishes to thank the Department, and also the European University Institute, for their support of the study on which the text is based.

form, while others were only provisionally sketched in. An outline of the themes he intended to cover will be found here, in the section entitled The Argument Continued.

Chapter 1 of the present text relates the experience of the 1960s and early 1970s, when – despite gloomy predictions – the Western-style economies (including Japan) continued to grow at an accelerated pace.

In the wake of the 1973 oil shock, uncertainties began to set in. Serious doubts about economic and social policy gained ground during the latter half of the decade as two business cycles unfolded. The countervailing effects of a demand for growth at the same time as increased welfare expenditure also made themselves felt. Economists and politicians alike, unable to manipulate with sufficient delicacy the tools of 'fine tuning', chose deliberate abstention in the hope of allowing market forces to reassert themselves. The theory of Nemesis on which this choice was based is discussed in Chapter 2.

The alternative approaches to economic decision-making – the neo-Keynesian one and the non-interventionist – are examined in Chapter 3, in terms of their costs and of the benefits they confer, against the background of the great variations of recent economic performance in individual Western countries and in Japan.

The overall theme was still a developing one. The advent of Reaganism in November 1980, with its consistent testing out of monetarist policies, would have added point to much of the argument and provided further illustrative material. What follows in this introduction has been compiled in large measure from Andrew Shonfield's own notes. It is intended as a backcloth to his text in its present form.

Andrew Shonfield's *Modern Capitalism,* published in 1965, marked the high point of an economic crest. Up to the mid-1960s the business cycle was being successfully controlled by governments which had increasingly large resources to dispose of, as well as a growing understanding of the working of the economic system. Fluctuations in business activity and employment were relatively modest. Medium-term planning, allied to sensitive short-term policies, resulted in a less wasteful use of productive capacity and therefore tended to make for a higher rate of return on investment. Moreover, the accelerating pace of technological innovation was thought to be likely to offset the forces that might contribute to a slowdown in economic growth. However, this vantage point was soon to prove not securely based.

By the mid-sixties the new fashions in economic thinking were beginning to spread – opposed to Keynesian doctrines, to government intervention by regulation, and, above all, to fast-growing public expenditure. Charles Kindleberger in his 1966 review of *Modern Capitalism* summed up the changing viewpoints of his fellow economists, asserting that '. . . supergrowth is over, and there is nothing that planning can do to restore it'.[2] In the event he was proved wrong about European growth rates; they continued high for the remainder of the sixties and into the early seventies.

It is in the United States – with its relatively low growth rate and growing reaction against the assertive interventionism of the L. B. Johnson Administration – and also in Britain that the confidence in the possibilities of 'fine tuning' showed the deepest marks of erosion. And suspicions regarding 'fine tuning' fostered a cult of economic non-interventionism. The intellectual basis for this mood is most liberally provided by the school of thought associated with Milton Friedman. It aims to stop politicians from trying to change the pace of economic activity – or its content – and to persuade them, in one of Friedman's phrases, 'to set the dials of the economy once and for all and then to walk away'.

There are other versions of the attempt to separate economics from politics which the author examined in terms of their institutional consequences. The notion of some independent or quasi-independent institution inside the apparatus of government which is concerned with the long-term interests of the economy is a familiar one in the Western world. An interesting variation on it, which emerged during the early post-war period in Europe, was the central planning commission, pioneered by France and adopted in a number of other countries. Part of its function was to ride over the oscillations in short-term economic policy, engaging private businesses and public agencies in commitments which tied them for several years. The planners had a varying record of success in different countries during the 1960s and 1970s; but only in few places, to some extent in France and more clearly in Japan (and even here the success needs to weather a longer period before it is proved conclusively), did they in practice achieve any very high degree of independence from the short-term objectives of the government of the day.

In the recent period the cherished instrument of independence in several countries has been the central bank. It is thought of by some as a model on which other institutions could be constructed, in order to control the propensity of politicians to prefer short-term to long-term interests. But not politicians only. Part of the interest in this line of thinking, which may be important for the future management of Western economies, is the view that the existence of institutions over which voters know that they *cannot* exercise direct control – like courts of law – is essential to the efficient functioning of modern democracy. Without it – to use old-fashioned phraseology – there is no means of curbing the impulses of the mob.

The significance of this line of reasoning – which, it is evident, bears a resemblance to the classical justification for the separation of powers – is that it is in marked contrast to the ideology which so powerfully influenced the early post-war period. In the first twenty years or so following the war the emphasis in public policy-making in so many Western countries was on the securing of the maximum degree of *integration* of public and private power. The answer to the problem of achieving high growth and a better distribution of wealth was believed to lie in the mobilization of all available sources of influence and power, in the public and private sectors, in pursuit of a number of rationally planned objectives. Indicative planning was seen as the means of marrying the private with the public. But if the central apparatus of the state is now deemed to have become so vulnerable to the accidents of reinforced and increasingly efficient popular pressures on government, then this weakness may decisively reduce the capacity of traditional government authority to act as the source of rational economic policy-making. What is to be put in its place? The old Keynesian ideology simply assumed the coherent working of public institutions. Can this coherence be reasserted and, if so, how will that affect the political assumptions underlying the relationship between the governors and the governed in a participatory type of democracy?

One consequence of the change of mood is, paradoxically, the renewed emphasis on *effective authority* in the thinking about the reform of public institutions. If economic variables cannot be reliably manipulated to produce the desired short-term results, then laws, threats, as well as more novel instruments of persuasion, have to be deployed. Depending on the particular doctrines of the policy-makers, these instruments will range from further, and more direct, monetary pressures to such consensual measures as wages and incomes policies.

A dramatic change of climate in the thinking of social scientists, policy-makers, and administrators such as characterized the period from the mid-sixties onwards is not a phenomenon without recent precedents. Back in the mid-1950s, Andrew Shonfield had written of the crude *laissez-faire* views of British Treasury officials: 'Rarely . . . can the doctrine of *anti-planning* have been carried to this degree of excess and the new philosophers, it is to be observed, were the same people who had carried out the Labour policies of state intervention during the period 1945–51.'[3] However, the mood which revealed itself in the second half of the 1960s was much more radical. What he saw now was a far-reaching backlash against a wide range of political and social tenets, and most particularly against the social welfare expansion of the earlier 1960s.

The beginning of the 1970s saw a growing revolt against high public expenditure, as well as the paradox of diminished confidence in the ability of governments to govern, coupled, in seeming contradiction, with demands for further and more effective government action – more extensive use of public power to cope with new problems, or with old ones which appeared to become more pressing.

In this welter of contradictory tendencies, which was by now most apparent in Western Europe, how far did essentially ideological considerations about the role of the State dominate policy? Was it merely a coincidence that so many of the economic policy-makers in so many different places thought that in the battle to control inflation the prime target was curbing the relative share of public expenditure? Or was there some deeper motivation deriving from a longer historical process? To put the point starkly: was the underlying political force a widely held belief that the advance of social welfare had already gone too far and that the attack on publicly induced inflation was one way of putting this activity back in its place?

On this reading of events, the persistence of inflation and, when it reached annual percentage rates of or approaching double fig-ures, the popular reaction to it, offered politicians of a conserva-tive cast a heaven-sent opportunity to set about the business of reversing the process which had largely occupied the domestic pol-icies of the countries of the Western world – when they were not fighting one another – ever since the early 1930s. Much of the early period since the end of the Second World War can perhaps be regarded as one of taking up and completing the unfinished business implicit in the libertarian movement of the early 1920s the Weimar Republic is the obvious point of reference, as sym-bolic of the spirit rather than as a clear expression of practice – and in the radical-egalitarian spirit underlying some of the re-forms of the 1930s. In its post-war manifestation, this spirit ex-pressed itself in a wide range of measures, backed by public inter-vention, ranging from 'affirmative action' legislation to the recognition of collective obligation to provide welfare services to the disadvantaged. The spreading doubts about the overwhelming presence of what Bernard Cazes has called 'l'Etat-protecteur'[4] came later and were closely allied to the idea of excessive public ex-penditure.

The share of output absorbed by public expenditure was cer-tainly expanding on a vast scale (in part at least to meet the de-mands of the very people who considered themselves to be subject to excessive government intervention). To some extent this was simply a continuation of a trend which had been in progress from the 1950s onwards. But two things made the situation different. The rate of increase at the end of the 1960s accelerated; during the seven years up to the mid-1970s the OECD countries on av-erage devoted an extra 1 per cent of their national product each year to the *purposes of public spending*.[5] Secondly, by the second half of the 1970s, the share of output taken by governments and their agencies amounted on average in the OECD group to over two-fifths of the total. Assuming that there is a limit beyond which public expenditure's share can only grow further on the basis of a drastic re-ordering of established views about the rights of citizens to decide the private uses of the bulk of their personal earnings, then many of these countries were visibly approaching it.

In fact, the share of public expenditure continued to increase for the remainder of the decade. It is a notable feature of the story of the rise that different groups of countries keep more or less the same place in the international league tables from the mid-1950s onwards.[6] Some part of the expansion in public expenditure reflected the efforts of governments, especially marked in the small, rich, successful countries of Western Europe, to counter the effects of recession and the business slowdown by additional government spending. But the main factor was the relentless advance in welfare provision, deriving in considerable measure from programmes of improvement decided on in principle in the past, and coming up for progressive implementation in conditions which were less favourable than those envisaged when the decisions were taken. They chiefly took the form of direct income transfers to the old, the sick, and to other categories of disadvantaged members of society. And, by and large, what the disadvantaged got in *real terms* was not an increasingly high proportion of the national product: the prices of many, labour-intensive, welfare services rose relatively more than other costs.[7]

There is no clear evidence that a high rate of increase in expenditure on welfare invariably correlates with a strong reaction against governments responsible for large-scale public expenditure. The northern group of small countries experienced the swiftest increase, and seemed to acquiesce in the process with little evidence of discomfort. At any rate, changes of government did not make any noticeable difference to the rising trend; nor did voters (except for a time in Denmark) apparently expect them to do so. Welfare spending was not a major issue in the reversals suffered by the ruling social democrat parties in Sweden and elsewhere during the 1970s. When, right at the end of the decade, decisions were at last made to cut back the share of public spending in the national product, it was less a matter of political choice than a generally recognized national need for coping with a long-term budgetary and balance of payments problem. In short, the small countries had banked on a return to a high rate of world economic growth which would have relieved the strain both on their budgets and their balance of payments, and when it became apparent, with the onset of the second business recession of the decade in 1979/80, that this hope was false, economic policies were changed. The political argument was primarily about who should sacrifice what; there was little serious argument about the requirement itself.

This was a very different situation from that in the United States and Britain, where public expenditure had become a major political issue. The British story, it should be said, has some very special features, since the Conservative Government which took power in 1979 offered its policy of cutting public expenditure as a remedy for the particular failure of Britain's economic performance by comparison with that of other Western countries during the previous quarter of a century. It was no part of the British Conservative argument that it was offering a model of behaviour which was applicable to all nations everywhere.

Of the two, the US reaction is of particular importance. The question that it raises is whether it presages a new mood which is likely to take hold more generally in the Western world. It was a strongly held view of Andrew Shonfield that such a mood, based on the nostalgia of the new generation of hard-money economists, is not a serious *longer-term* option in contemporary society. 'We have gone too far in the other direction to be able to reverse the assumptions which millions of workers now take for granted about the tolerable limits of discomfort within which society works, unless there is a major political upheaval. What has to be understood is that there is no substitute for politics. The monetarists, who purport to have found one, simply assume that the voters and the politicians whom they elect will, if they are pushed, both recognize the monetarists' own particular version of the ineluctable!'[8]

He himself did not believe that purely doctrinal solutions would succeed in resolving the economic problems of the period to come. While he realized that 'there is no possible escape from the business of "day-to-day management" of the economy',[9] his thinking was dominated by the 'seeming paradox' of the modern state, which had been forced to recognize the limits of its capacity for short-term management, being 'called upon increasingly to take charge of its long-term management. These are, however, entirely different functions requiring very different skills and techniques of intervention. The pretensions of the omnicompetent state have gone. But the interventionist state is more necessary than ever.' [10]

How to modify the institutions of the interventionist state so as to make them responsive to the needs of the disadvantaged members of society had been the subject of the last chapter of *Modern Capitalism*. How to protect the public institutions themselves from the tyranny of majority pressure groups was the problem which, in the last weeks of his working life, he identified as the most important challenge of the period to come.

I approach the usually pleasurable task of thanking those whose help has made this book possible with mixed feelings. I have received the support and encouragement of many individuals and several institutions through the half-year of editorial work. But I realize how inadequate my words of appreciation must needs be in encompassing all the teaching, inspiration, and advice – and also the practical help – that Andrew had from numerous friends and colleagues. I put my faith in the knowledge that those whom I omit – not through indifference or negligence, but because of ignorance or fallible memory – will be magnanimous about the omissions. Only Andrew would have been able to do everyone full justice.

Many may be disappointed not to find in this book any direct traces of the exchanges of views they had with the author over the years. They will remember, I feel sure, that the present text is of necessity a synthesis of some of the ideas only. Many other ideas have been transmitted in lectures and seminars to a wide circle of economists and political scientists working on allied subjects, and have already borne fruit through their writing and teaching.

Andrew began planning and researching the material for 'Modern Capitalism Two' (his working title for the new study) while he was still at Chatham House. The research committee of the Royal Institute of International Affairs, under the guidance of Alan Bullock, criticized and encouraged the work at the preparatory stage. The committee's advice and support laid solid foundations for the entire project.

The preliminary researches for a complex scheme such as was originally envisaged required much study in several of the countries under analysis. In the autumn of 1976 we spent four months in the United States, where Andrew held a fellowship at the Woodrow Wilson International Center for Scholars in Washington. The hospitality of James Billington and his staff, and the stimulating exchanges with the Center's Fellows, were backed up by a series of seminar encounters at the Council on Foreign Relations in New York. Under the chairmanship of William Diebold, Andrew's preliminary conclusions about the future of the mixed economy were subjected to detailed scrutiny in five lively discussions. A third American body, the Brookings Institution, also contributed materially to Andrew's thinking. At Brookings he found an awareness of the necessary interaction between economic theory and practical policy-making which closely corresponded to his own intellectual tastes.

As the ideas for 'Modern Capitalism Two' began to take shape Andrew became aware that the Japanese economy, deliberately omitted in the earlier study, would figure prominently in his reexamination of the balance of public and private power. His two-month stay in Tokyo was funded by a Nissan Fellowship, through the good offices of Takeshi Watanabe and Tadashi Yamamoto at the Japan Center for International Exchange. The experience allowed both of us to acquire first-hand knowledge and make many valued friendships and contacts. A seminar hosted by Masahide Shibusawa, at which Kinhide Mushakoji, Kazuo Nukazawa, Saburō Okita, and Tadashi Yamamoto were present, was a major contribution to Andrew's analysis of the Japanese economic scene. His conclusions were later summarized at a useful encounter with the Japanese employers' association, the Keidanren, early in September 1979.

Other series of international encounters have, I know, contributed materially to the shaping of Andrew's thinking. Among the most useful were the meetings of the Villa Pamphilli group of economists engaged in the study of international monetary affairs and the discussions in 1980 with French planners preparatory to his critique of the VIIIth Plan.

I come now to the body of special friends at the European University Institute, whose first Principal, Max Kohnstamm, persuaded Andrew to come to Florence to teach and write about the mixed economy. I shared the support, advice, and friendship of Andrew's colleagues at the EUI, and they continued to guide and encourage me when I took over the task of editing the manuscripts he had left. Each of these individuals merits more space than I have at my disposal here. The past and present members of the Economics Department, and its two heads, Jean-Paul Fitoussi and Marcello de Cecco, deserve particular thanks, on behalf of Andrew and also of myself. Without the patient and good-humoured help of Jacqueline Bourgonje, Andrew's writing would have been difficult and my own work impossible. I owe a special debt to Wolfgang Hager; on a number of occasions he saved my ideas from running aground, and yet made me feel that the steering remained in my own hands.

These colleagues are part of a group of intimate and long-standing friends. With Bernard Cazes, William Diebold Jnr., François Duchêne, Arthur Knight, Arrigo Levi, John Pinder, Kurt Richebächer, Pierre Salmon, and Niels Thygesen, their discussions with Andrew over many years helped in the formulation of ideas which led to this book. Several of them also contributed in great measure to the planning and editing of its contents. Andrew would have thanked all these friends more specifically and adequately than I can, but at least I can say that I share the special friendship he felt for them.

It goes without saying that I am most grateful to John Hicks for what he has said in the Foreword to this book; it would have made Andrew very proud to have him write it.

Three librarians were particularly helpful at different stages in the preparation of material for this text: Dorothy Hamerton at Chatham House, Zdenko David at the Woodrow Wilson Center, and Michiel Tegelaars at the European University. Bonnie Bonis helped me a great deal by her special ability in deciphering

Andrew's handwriting. On several occasions when I despaired of finding references for the text, Peter Versteeg produced facts and figures with the greatest expedition and a minimum of fuss.

I could not have performed the task of editing his work without the long years of learning by Andrew's side. Any failures are due to my shortcomings as a student, not to any incapacity of his as a teacher. He would, I think, have wanted the *complete* work to be dedicated to his colleagues at the European University Institute. For my part, I would like to dedicate my share of the work to our son David and daughter Katherine, in recognition of the support I derived from Katherine's encouragement and from David's skilled editorial assistance, critical ability, and sense of shape.

September 1981   ZUZANNA SHONFIELD

THE USE OF PUBLIC POWER

1

The Age of Acceleration

Groping for the shape of contemporary history, one finds quite often that one's memory responds as if it was affected by a mild form of sclerosis. The most distant events are clear and distinct; one can even recite, in sclerotic style, the equivalent of complicated verses about them retained from the clarity of childhood. But the more recent past, especially the middle distance, is clouded; the patterns, more complicated and varied in texture, are easily lost. It is much the same with folk-memory. So it should perhaps come as no surprise that there is little popular awareness of the turmoil of the period of the 1960s which forms a kind of prelude to the present study – no feeling for the upheavals which accompanied the onrush of affluence and for the marked acceleration of the pace of change which took hold of the Western world. From the standpoint of a later age, which has experienced the new uncertainties that emerged from the mid-1970s onwards, it looks like a remarkably stable, unruffled time.

It was not. At the start of the period there was anxiety about the future. By the end of the 1950s widespread doubt was being expressed about whether the great economic expansion associated with the post-war reconstruction of shattered societies in Europe and Japan, together with the revival of long-suppressed business energies, could be sustained at anything like the pace so far achieved. It was to be expected that the wholesale removal of the shackles on enterprise and trade inherited from the 1930s would elicit a response, and that this would be reinforced by a catching-up process as the rest of the world outside North America absorbed the simpler innovative improvements in efficiency and productive power pioneered by the Americans. A pause of some kind was thought to be in the likely order of events. The long-term historical evidence seemed to suggest that conclusion. To quote from one careful survey of the record of the 1950s in the context of the economic history of the previous century, published at this time: 'Though nothing exceptional or unprecedented has happened yet, it will be unprecedented if the rapid post-war rates are continued for another ten or fifteen years. . . .'[1] That was on the basis of developments up to 1959. In the event a further fourteen years of even faster economic growth followed. The above conclusion was based on a comparison of one long period before the First World War, including the last part of the nineteenth century, with the four and a half decades following 1914. For several industrial countries the average rate of growth in the first period was somewhat higher than in the second; moreover some countries had experienced occasional short bursts of expansion, either before or after the First World War, in which they had reached or surpassed the rapid rate of growth of 1950–9. By and large, the story suggested that the nations of the Western world had got back on course by the late 1950s and that this had involved a spectacular and sustained sprint at the end. It would be foolhardy to suppose that the latter could be continued. Indeed, there were already some indications that the pace was beginning to tail off.

The continuities of Western economic behaviour, viewed in a longer time perspective, were still being stressed by commentators in the 1960s. Peter Drucker, a perceptive analyst of contemporary economic trends, made much of these in a book tracing developments up to the middle of the decade.[2] In spite of the disruption of two world wars and the long depression of the 1930s, the average annual rate of growth over the fifty years after 1914 had not, he averred, changed significantly from the rate established before the First World War. Nor had the international economic structure altered. Even the identity of the leading industrial nations was the same – no new member had 'joined the club' in the half century between the outbreak of the First World War and the middle-1960s. Most strikingly, Drucker argued, any economist who had simply extrapolated the long-term economic trends apparent in 1914 and then returned to measure the outcome fifty years later would have found that he had achieved a remarkably accurate forecast: '. . . by the mid-sixties all economically advanced countries had, on the whole, reached the levels of production and income they would have attained had the economic trends of the thirty or so years *before* 1914 continued, basically unchanged, for another fifty years.'[3]

The experience of the individual nations which make up the advanced industrial world differs greatly and it is hard to subject a large aggregative statement of this kind to critical assessment. It so happens that the United States for rather special reasons performed very well indeed during the period just before the First World War, the period of mass immigration and the advancing frontier of the national economy, but did less well than others subsequently. Germany and Japan did relatively better in the half century after 1914, and outstandingly better after the Second World War. How is one to weight these performances in order to arrive at a precise date on which Peter Drucker's doctrine of long-term continuity in underlying economic trends could be proved true or false? There is no entirely satisfactory way of doing this.[4] A reasonable, though necessarily approximative, reading of the available statistical data shows that around the year 1960 most of the advanced industrial countries were at or above the economic level that they would have reached if the trend of annual economic growth established during the prosperous period preceding the First World War had continued. The question then is whether any significance attaches to the fact that the high growth in the favourable conditions immediately following the Second World War counterbalanced the effects of disaster and depression in the previous quarter of a century. Were these simply two mutually offsetting quirks in a system guided by deep forces making for a steady norm? One way of seeking an answer is to see what happened next.

Productivity and Full Employment

Drucker's observation does, indeed, serve to draw attention to the fact that it was after the industrial nations of the West had got back, around 1960, to the point where a steady continuation of the long-term trend would have taken them, that the trend-line of economic growth shifted markedly upwards. Moreover this happened in circumstances where all previous historical experience would have pointed to the prospect of a slowdown, not an acceleration. It came after quite a long period of rapid expansion, especially in Europe, during which the available productive capacities, including unemployed labour, had been largely absorbed. Except in North America, there was full, or nearly full, employment – as measured by the conventional criteria of the time: under 3 per cent unemployed in Europe and under 2 per cent in Japan. What made the performance that followed in the non-American world uniquely different from that of other periods of rapid growth was that, starting out from record levels of employment, with economies operating close to full stretch *on the basis of existing capacity,* output was boosted by a marked acceleration in the advance of labour productivity lasting for a whole decade. It is worth noting that the unusually rapid increase in output per person employed during this period was accompanied by a marked decline in the average number of hours worked in Western Europe and Japan. The reduction in working time was extremely sharp in some of the most rapidly growing countries, amounting to some 8 per cent by the end of the decade in Germany and Sweden.[5] Thus output per man-hour increased even more rapidly than individual productivity.

The United States' experience was in this, as in other respects, different from the rest of the industrial world. There was no spurt in the pace of growth of productivity and there was no reduction in average working time. The marked increase in the rate of growth of production from the early 1960s onwards derived entirely from putting more people to work. American unemployment was high at the end of the 1950s, and its reduction was one of the main purposes of the Democratic administrations which managed the economy during most of the 1960s. During the early stages of the long boom which followed, US productivity continued to increase moderately, in line with long-term trends. Even without a special spurt of the kind achieved in Europe and Japan, American output per worker was in absolute terms significantly larger than that of the other advanced industrial countries.[6]

In the second half of the 1960s the United States diverged even further from the economic trends which took over in the other advanced industrial countries. While the expansion of output continued, reinforced by the mounting demands of the Vietnam War, there was a marked decline in the rate of growth of productivity.[7] This happened to coincide with the widening impulse of President Johnson's 'Great Society' social reform programmes as they spread through the American community. The size and speed of this major social change may, in conjunction with the large-scale American war effort, have produced some unfavourable economic side-effects. It should be remembered that it was a conscious aim of the programme of social reform not only to create job opportunities for groups that had previously been passed by; there was the more ambitious objective of creating a new confidence among these people, members of racial minorities, women and other underprivileged workers, which would prompt them to demand as of right better terms from their employers than the latter had been ready to concede to them in the past. The result, at least in certain parts of the economy, had something of the character of an upheaval. It is normally found that during the upward phase of a business cycle, when the pressure of demand is rising, productivity tends to move up faster – for a variety of reasons. Among these is the obvious one that during a boom the average worker's time is more fully employed. On this occasion there was no such benefit; and an analysis of the data has suggested the explanation that the normally favourable business-cycle effect was entirely offset by the lower quality of the workers brought into employment in the second half of the 1960s.[8] If so, this would have to count, at any rate in part, as an economic penalty for the long-delayed effort followed by sudden action to remove the social disadvantages imposed on large groups of people, especially blacks, who had been treated as marginal to the main body of the nation.

Even so, this does not provide a complete explanation of why the United States, which was endowed with a much more plentiful supply of labour than the other major industrial areas, gained so little relative advantage from it. The differences were enormous: the US labour force increased by 18.6 million between 1960 and 1973, a rise of more than one quarter, while in Western Europe, despite the large influx of immigrant labour from neighbouring countries, the total population of working age hardly increased at all. Yet the US economy seemed to be affected earlier than the economies of Europe by the manpower constraint and to feel it more keenly, as the economic expansion proceeded towards its climax in 1973.

The point emerges even more sharply from a comparison of the American case with that of Japan. The Japanese benefited throughout this period from the demographic trends which brought large cohorts of the population to working age, at a time when the birth rate was undergoing a marked and apparently permanent decline. The consequent expansion of the work force (by 18 per cent from 1960 to 1973) was reflected in the absence of any noticeable constraint on the supply of labour despite the pressure of an exceptionally rapid rate of economic growth. It was also accompanied by a rapid and sustained increase in productivity.[9] One can only speculate about the underlying causes of the American phenomenon. It seems to be associated with a more general difficulty of the US economy in reducing its 'hard core' of unemployment, even during periods of boom, to levels which West Europeans and Japanese would regard as socially tolerable. Is this problem, both in its earlier manifestation in the 1960s and during the boom of the late 1970s, a reflection of a much more heterogeneous society where a basic industrial culture is more unevenly spread? Or is it rather that the main source of the problem is that the high US standards of productivity – still markedly higher, it should be emphasized again, than the European and Japanese – mean that more people are unable to meet the demanding standards of normal work performance? It might of course be that both causes were present and in combination made matters worse. But it is worth noting that if the second cause is significant then the Europeans and the Japanese, as they reach the already established levels of American productivity, are likely in turn to face the prospects of an enlarged hard core of unemployment even during periods of high prosperity.

However, during the great expansion of the 1960s there was no sign of any such tendency in Western Europe, where the supply of new labour was meagre and where unemployment remained on average very low, while economic growth was not significantly constrained by labour shortage. The explanation in large part was that European workers proved unexpectedly mobile, showing a readiness to leave jobs, and places in which they and their families had been long established, in response to new employment opportunities. The big spurt in productivity reflected some of these large changes in the structure of production and employment. There was a myth which became current during the economic slowdown of the second half of the 1970s that problems of 'structural change' were a special burden of the new age which had arrived with the oil crisis and its aftermath. But all that had really happened was that a silent and very profound shift in the pattern of employment, which had accelerated like nearly everything else after 1960, was in prospect of being succeeded by other changes, not necessarily more severe or far-reaching but much less silent in their operation. This is essentially another way of saying that they would be taking place in an economic context in which full employment had ceased to be the norm.

Social Costs of New Employment Patterns

Nevertheless, the structural shift in employment which took 6.7 million West Europeans out of agricultural occupations between 1960 and 1973 was the kind of change which was bound, at any time, to put a strain on the social system.[10] The change of occupation which in agriculture normally involved both a shift in location and an alteration in an established way of life affected some 7 per cent of the total employed population of this area – a number equal to the employed population of Sweden and Denmark combined. It was not that the transfer produced unhappiness: the outcome was for the vast majority of those involved an improvement in their material standard of living. But that should not obscure the fact that it was perceived by the great majority of those

who moved as a radical decision involving personal and social
risks – especially perhaps for members of their families whom they
left behind. The effort by governments to ease this process, and
especially to safeguard the living standards of those who would
still be working on the land after the mass exodus, had a large
measure of success. The rapid rise in agricultural productivity which
took place at the same time was a help here. But the smooth conduct of the operation required active intervention by governments
and a generous outpouring of public funds. One of its heritages is
the European Community's Common Agricultural Policy, with the
follies which have become the scandal of a later generation – only
matched by comparable financial extravagance in countries like
Japan which experienced a similar exodus. It is perhaps not surprising that governments faced with a structural change of this
magnitude were inclined to over-insure against the economic and
social risks.

There were other structural shifts affecting whole communities
of workers just as profound as those affecting agriculture, though
on a smaller scale. Even so, the numbers were not insignificant. In
European coal-mining over three-quarters of a million workers lost
their jobs and the number employed in the industry was more
than halved in a dozen years up to 1973. The decline in the textile
and clothing industries was less dramatic, but here again one and
a quarter million people lost their jobs and had to find employment elsewhere. In general it was the traditional industries dating
from the early stages of the industrial revolution, in which the
social bonds of work were often especially strong, which were
wrenched apart by the wind of change which swept across the
Western world during the years of high prosperity. Railways were
an outstanding example, and the shock here was reinforced by the
fact that railway employment had for long been regarded as particularly respectable and safe.[11] Within manufacturing industry
there were significant shifts in employment, especially in the latter
stages of the period up to 1973. Indeed from 1970 onwards total
factory employment in Western Europe declined, in spite of the
hectic pace of economic expansion during the final boom. In this
sense the early 1970s were a kind of slow prelude to the much
more rapid movement which occurred later.

The structural change which was characteristic of this epoch naturally affected the ownership and management of business firms as well as the jobs of employees. Here too there is evidence of acceleration compared with the 1950s. It was at the top end of the European economy, where real output and income per capita were highest, that the development was most visible. In Sweden for example the number of firms closing down each year during the 1960s was three times as great as during the previous decade; at the same time take-overs and mergers of firms influenced the prospects of an estimated 3–5 per cent of the Swedish labour force each year, compared with 1 per cent previously.[12] The Swedish case lends further support to the general conclusion reached in a study of the pattern of economic change in the European Community, from which the earlier data on employment are derived. It observed 'a very close link between the scale of the changes and the rate of overall growth. The countries enjoying the highest growth rates were also those in which changes in the production apparatus were most far-reaching. Conversely, the United Kingdom experienced both slow growth and insignificant changes in its production structure. . . .'[13]

Surveying the economic performance of the epoch of expansion, there is nothing in the story which lends support to the dire criticisms of the full-employment policies of the time which were made by Professor Hayek, and which acquired a degree of popularity in the mood of doom and doubt of the 1970s and early 1980s, on the ground that the inflexibility built into such policies made them self-destructive. Writing in the late 1960s he asserted: 'Full employment policies, as at present practised, attempt the quick and easy way of giving men employment where they happen to be, while the real problem is to bring about a distribution of labour which makes continuous high employment without artificial stimulus possible.'[14] His prediction was that the very intensity with which nations sought to achieve high employment would lead to higher levels of unemployment later on. Hence his popular appeal at a time when unemployment seemed to be inexorably on the increase. In fact, however, the experience of the 1960s suggests that the pursuit of high employment is in no way incompatible with a flexible response to changes in demand. Countries which achieved the *lowest* rates of unemployment in the 1960s, like Germany and Austria, not only adapted their economic structures to secure very rapid growth during the boom, but also managed to maintain employment and economic activity during the period of difficulty which followed at a higher level than other countries. The contrast with the United States, which persistently lagged behind the successful European countries, both in the pace of economic growth and in the reduction of unemployment during the 1960s, is striking.

International Trade: Rewards and Risks

The change in the structure of production was matched by a parallel shift in the market outlets of the goods and services produced by the advanced industrial countries. Again, Hayek and his school predicted a profound mismatch between the greatly enlarged productive capacity, created in the era of high employment, and the requirements of potential customers around the world. 'It seems highly doubtful', he wrote in the same essay as that quoted above, 'whether the expansionist policies pursued since the War in most countries have helped and not rather hindered that adjustment to radically changed conditions of world trade which has become necessary. . . .' [15] In fact during the 1960s, more than ever before, the industrial countries systematically opened up their domestic markets to competition from abroad and at the same time sharply increased the share of their production directed towards export trade. There was indeed a spirit almost of recklessness about the way in which these nations hastened to make their well-being, and even their livelihood, more and more dependent on the decisions of foreign governments and people, with little regard for the risk that there might be times when the latter would lack either the resources or the desire to buy the products on offer.

Probably the most severe test of the willingness to adapt to changing conditions of international trade was the reaction to the growing exports of manufactured goods from the newly industrializing countries of the Third World, from the early 1960s onwards. A study by the OECD of this increasingly important segment of international trade recorded a variety of forms of resistance put up by the rich countries to the penetration of their markets by these thrusting and efficient newcomers. Their total share of Western markets remained relatively modest. However, the pace of advance in particular categories of products and in individual Western markets was fast enough to cause problems. The study noted that the responses, in the form of changes in the structure of Western business and employment to accommodate this trade, were more rapid during the 1960s – 'at a time when manufacturing employment was still increasing in most countries' – than they became later on. In the 1970s, as the Western world has moved away from full employment, this 'structure has become somewhat more rigid'.[16]

The relationship with this group of highly successful developing countries has to be seen in the context of a larger geographical shift in the distribution of world industrial production, with a declining share of the total going to the older centres in Western Europe and North America. In this case too the big shift began in the early 1960s and gathered momentum from then on. During the first stage of the post-war economic revival before that, which was dominated by an extremely dynamic Western Europe, what occurred was essentially a consolidation of the earlier international distribution of industrial power, pivoted on the North Atlantic area. At this stage Japan and the group of advanced developing countries (identified in note n. 16, p. 119) accounted together for some 10 per cent of the world's industrial production. Then in the course of little more than a dozen years that share increased to 18 per cent, while the proportion of Europe and North America combined fell by an equivalent amount.[17] This extraordinary growth of production in the newer industrial centres was accompanied by an even more rapid increase in the export of manufactures to the older developed countries. Meanwhile the latter continued to make gains in their output and trade despite the pressure from their more dynamic rivals. But it required a stepped-up pace of adaptation. This is reflected in the acceleration of the so-called 'product cycle' of which there is evidence from the early 1960s onwards – that is to say, a shorter time interval between the development of new products, their marketing abroad, and finally the establishment of rival sources of production outside the country which was the original source of the innovation.[18] Behind this process there were a number of forces leading to an acceleration of the transfer of technology from the most advanced countries to others. Information was more rapidly and cheaply available; transport costs were low so that it would pay to set up new sources of production in places where labour was relatively cheap and plentiful; and, perhaps most important, exports from the older industrial countries of machinery embodying the most up-to-date technology were growing at a great pace. Thus there was a built-in tendency for innovations to spread faster; moreover, the large multinational companies which became increasingly active at this stage provided an especially efficient vehicle.

This story draws attention once again to the considerable risks inherent in the strategy of the old-established industrial countries making foreign trade the hinge of economic growth. Why were the risks so blithely accepted? It was not as if export markets required less effort to penetrate or offered a higher rate of profit per unit sold – on the contrary, the evidence is that prices of goods exported were frequently pared down below those sold in the home market – and the foreign markets were certainly not more secure. If industrialists took into account the political influence that they might be able to exercise in any attempt to maintain their position in a period of business difficulty, it was obvious that, except in very special cases, they would have more chance of putting effective pressure on their own governments than on those abroad. However, what seems to have counted for more than these considerations was the general sentiment widely shared by the managers of large-scale industry about international trade as the motor of economic growth – that a sustained expansion of their home markets would occur only if accompanied by a still more rapid advance in international commerce. That at any rate seemed to reflect the experience of the mature economies in the first half of the twentieth century, with the possible exception of the United States during the 1920s. And indeed it took a little time after the Second World War before the American business community at large was persuaded of the proposition which seemed so obvious to its European counterparts. It was the US government, in part for long-term political reasons, which initially led the way; big business followed with rising enthusiasm as its operations became increasingly international.

It is noteworthy that the degree of emphasis on foreign trade in national policies was not directly correlated with success in export business. Germany, which became the world's largest exporter of manufactures in the 1960s, raised the share of its national product which was dependent on foreign trade by some 50 per cent in the course of ten years; and the proportion went on increasing during the 1970s. But this was not at all exceptional. Nor was the consequent change in the distribution of employment. During the ten years of high prosperity up to 1973 the number of industrial workers employed in meeting consumer demand in the home market decreased by 1.4 million, while employment in the export trades rose by 1.1 million.[19] By the late 1970s, when total employment in manufacturing industry had fallen off further, there were only two workers employed in consumer industries serving the home market for each one employed in the production of goods for foreign customers. These industries are of course especially vulnerable to short-term changes in taste and spending power.

Taking the whole field of international trade in goods and services, several other countries increased dependence on foreign markets (measured by their share of GNP) even more than the Germans; thus in the United States, where the share of foreign trade in the national product doubled between the early 1960s and the late 1970s. Here an explanation might be that the initial proportion of foreign trade was unusually low and that even at the end of the period it was only a little over 10 per cent. On the other hand the low Japanese proportion, some 12 per cent, hardly changed during the period. There may be some force in the notion that, during the period of high prosperity from the early 1960s onwards, there was a process of 'catching up' by some nations which had previously bought relatively little abroad and were now discovering the attractions of foreign-made goods and services. At the same time, the experience of the smaller industrial countries of Western Europe which were already thoroughly attuned, well before the 1960s, to a high degree of dependence on foreign trade suggests that this was not the whole story. These countries typically had a foreign trade sector which represented upwards of one-third of their national products; and that proportion increased markedly during our period, in some cases to nearly one-half.

The Japanese case emerges as a major exception, especially striking in view of its formidable performance as an exporter. Its relatively low ratio of foreign trade to GNP in part reflected a stubborn resistance, by contrast with other industrial nations, to the absorption of large quantities of foreign manufactures. The contrast was the more striking in view of the fact that the Japanese themselves depended for their extraordinary success in export markets on the progressive internationalization of tastes, of product design, and of wholesaleing and retailing, among the advanced industrial nations. It may be that one of the causes of Japan's exceptional behaviour in the 1960s and early 1970s was a certain lag in the perception of their own affluence. They continued for long to hold the traditional view of themselves as an essentially poor economy compelled to rely on foreigners for imports of 'necessities', notably energy and raw materials; anything else that they needed should so far as possible be manufactured at home. An alternative way of putting the point is to say that they believed it was a rational policy to insure against the uncertainties of foreign trade by limiting their dependence on imports wherever they could do so without economic damage to themselves.

It is useful to recall the Japanese experience, because it serves to underline the point that there was nothing inevitable about the world-wide conquest of markets by imported manufactured goods; with the appropriate institutions and policies, the process could after all be successfully impeded. There were of course particular economic interest groups in most countries which saw themselves ·being adversely affected by the hectic chase after foreign trade, but although protectionist attitudes and proposals quite often elicited popular clamour which was sometimes translated by governments into protectionist action, the mainstream of public policy moved powerfully in the opposite direction. There could hardly be a clearer proof of that fact than the figures cited earlier of the consistent increase in the proportion of internationally traded goods absorbed by the nations of the Western world. Such things do not happen by accident.

In some ways the most remarkable aspect of the resulting change in the economic substructure of the Western world is that its timing coincided with the rapid and decisive decline in the international political power of the West. This power had been greatly extended and then consolidated over most of the globe in the course of the colonial advance of the previous one and a half centuries. It then disappeared almost completely in a couple of decades. The presence of colonial authority, backed in the last resort by military force, at key points in the network of world commerce had provided a form of inexpensive insurance for those whose livelihood and comfort depended on international transactions. The number of the latter grew exceedingly just at the time that the system of insurance disappeared. The implications of the change were barely noticed, until the Arab oil embargo in 1973 brought it to public recognition.

Maintaining Open Markets

Yet it would be wrong to suppose that even that painful experience brought a decisive change in Western attitudes on this subject. Yes, some extra security in the form of additional reserves of oil in consuming countries was sought and partially obtained by the end of the 1970s; and a number of steps were taken to ensure that domestic production of energy would supply a rising proportion of needs in the long run. But the implicit thesis at the centre of Western policy, that almost anything was good so long as it added to the volume of foreign trade that exporters could compete for, was not seriously questioned. In searching for the reason why this was so, a half-dozen different explanations of a more or less psychological character, with varying admixtures of the irrational, readily suggest themselves. But before having recourse to these, there is one economic magnitude which expresses the peculiar character of the enhanced dependence on foreign decisions, which the Western nations accepted but over which they had no control: it merits attention because it points to the possibility of an explanation which is *not* devoid of rationality. This is that after more than thirty years of continuous expansion of the share of foreign trade in the economies of the advanced industrial countries of the OECD, that group still devoted only 5 per cent of its total expenditure to imports from nations outside the group.[20] It was to a very large extent a closed circle of exchanges with a few openings for outsiders. One of these, as we have seen, provided a channel of entry for the growing volume of cheap manufactured goods produced by the small group of advanced developing countries. This was managed in various ways, through such international devices as the Multi-fibre Arrangement of the GATT,[21] so that the balance between non-OECD supplies and domestic production was not seriously threatened.

The other element was imported oil. This was indeed an important form of economic dependence, and the development of this dependence – like almost everything else in the 1960s, proceeding at headlong speed – had been recklessly ignored by the West. But it had proved to be a solitary and special case: in spite of predictions of other disasters in the wake of the oil crisis of 1973,[22] there had been no scope in other commodities for comparable ventures in holding the West to ransom.

Thus the advanced industrial countries as a group are, as the OECD Secretariat observed, 'relatively self-contained'. That is reflected strikingly in the estimated effect of a proposed stimulus to demand, designed to overcome the economic slowdown of the late 1970s. This stimulus, the OECD was able to show, would be largely confined within the club to its own members, with a multiplier effect on their output of something over two and a half, and very little 'leakage' of the additional demand to the rest of the world, except to the oil-producing countries.[23] The significant fact which emerges from such calculations is that the increased risks apparently accepted by the Western nations in international trade turn out to have had a very special political connotation. They amounted essentially to a bet on the likely behaviour of fellow members of the OECD group, and of no one else. It was, all the same, the kind of bet which these nations would have hesitated to take in the context of the international politics of any earlier period, certainly that between the two world wars. What was implied first of all was an assumption that the constraints of international interdependence, and above all the avoidance of military action or the threat of it between themselves, were accepted by the members of the club of advanced industrial countries.

The second implicit assumption was less precise, though almost as important: that there was a high probability of reasonably competent political management of domestic affairs in the great majority of the member countries of the group. This was a necessary corollary to the first condition, if it was to be translated into decisions by businessmen about the probable international environment that would enable them to reap the benefits of the substantial and long-term investments which they had to make in order to secure the advantages of expanding foreign trade. It did not exclude the possibility – indeed it was highly probable – that individual governments would on occasion be guilty of gross mismanagement. But the implied calculation was that such disasters, if and when they occurred, would be contained, partly through the spirit of solidarity within the club and the help of the international institutions which the club, through its most powerful members, controlled.

It is not that these assumptions and their precise qualifications were consciously argued out during the age of accelerated expansion – only that they were implied by the behaviour of governments and businessmen. Moreover, there is some ambiguity about what the 'constraints of international interdependence' amount to in practice at any given time; there are different degrees of respect which they may be accorded and tacit conventions about the kind of disrespect that is tolerable or not.[24] What concerns us is the inference that may be drawn about the probable future behaviour of the group. The argument suggests that so long as the great majority of OECD countries, including the half-dozen big nations, continue to behave in a manner which does not increase the hazards, as perceived by others, of relying on them to maintain reasonably efficient and open markets for the sale of industrial goods (and also to provide ready access to foreign buyers of their products), there is no reason to expect that the liberal trend in policies governing international trade among advanced capitalist countries will be interrupted or reversed. 'Open markets' in this context means those in which the share of foreigners is not reduced in order to raise the share of domestic suppliers; it means giving the outsider an undiminished opportunity to capture the same proportionate share of additional purchases of industrial goods as he has enjoyed hitherto.

There is an important proviso about the nature of the risks perceived by those responsible for business decisions which deserves notice. Hitherto we have been considering deliberate action by national authorities designed to limit foreign access, and we have also confined it to industrial goods – on the assumption that continued discrimination against foreign suppliers of agricultural and other primary products in favour of domestic producers will not disrupt the system in the future, any more than it has in the past. Trade policy for manufactures, judging by the experience of the past thirty years, can apparently be kept in a largely watertight compartment. There is some occasional leakage, but not much. However, a sense of enhanced risk to industrial exporters may arise not as a result of some shift of policy in importing countries but because underlying economic circumstances change.

In a period of very slow growth, like the 1930s, international trade in manufactures lagged far behind the increase in production. Between 1929, the best year of the 1920s, and 1937, which was the high point of the recovery from the depression, world industrial output rose by one-tenth while international trade in manufactures only struggled back to a point 15 per cent below the 1929 level.[25] This was an extreme case, but it is not to be dismissed as a peculiar feature of an extraordinary depression. In the 1920s, even during the years of comparative prosperity from 1926 onwards, trade in manufactures had lagged markedly behind the rise in world production.[26] A variety of factors, including most especially the protectionist policies adopted by governments in that epoch of ultra-nationalism and mutual suspicion, caused the share of international trade in world production and sales of industrial goods to fall continuously.

If we look for evidence in more favourable times before the First World War, we find that international trade in manufactures moved broadly in line with world output, but no faster. W. A. Lewis argues on the basis of an elaborate, and persuasive, statistical analysis that the *value* of manufactures as a proportion of total world trade, at current prices, remained fairly constant for sixty years, from 1880 onwards.[27] The volume of industrial exports during this extended period depended chiefly on the terms of trade between primary products and manufactures. If world manufacturing output expanded, an increased proportion of it would be traded internationally only if the primary producers were doing well on the prices or the volume of their exportable production, or on both. They did best in fact when business in the industrial countries was booming and demand for commodities was strong. The rise and fall of the spendable incomes of primary producers determined the structure of international trade in other goods: they spent as much as they earned. Then this neat relationship changed following the Second World War because, as Lewis puts it, the industrial countries 'reduced their barriers against importing from each other, which had mounted continually from 1880 to 1950'.[28] The primary producers lost their dominant economic influence just when the industrial countries lost their colonial power. Both were liberated – though the developing countries have felt cheated ever since.

Lewis's observation on the great statistical change which occurred after 1950 – he calls it 'a fickle event' – draws attention once again to the decisive importance of government policy decisions in the process of international trade. Governments which had for sixty years (from 1880 to the Second World War) acted for the most part – there were exceptions – in one way, then acted for thirty years in an opposite way, to make themselves more and more dependent on the markets of other nations. (One wonders what would have happened if their post-war decisions in the matter had been subject to a series of popular referenda.) In the middle and late 1970s the proportion of international trade consisting of exchanges between industrial countries has declined and so has the ratio of the growth of trade in manufactures to manufacturing output.[29] Growth of trade is still a multiple of the growth of output, but a smaller one. These few years are much too short a period to establish a change of trend; but they serve to emphasize the fragile character of some of the tacit assumptions which have provided the foundation for confident policies. The factor to which it is worth drawing attention in the story of the *voluntary* increase of dependence on foreign trade is the primacy of the political condition. It was the consolidation of that condition during the 1960s which contributed largely to the extraordinary pace of advance in the period *after* the end of post-war reconstruction.

Private Affluence and Public Welfare

The main thesis of this chapter is that the developments which we have seen at work in international trade – an acceleration of the tempo of change, a more confident attitude to the resulting affluence, reflected in turn in a bolder approach to policy-making – were part of a larger phenomenon which occurred in a variety of fields of economic and social activity at about the same time. It affected attitudes to sex, to crime, to legal punishments – this was the time when the death penalty effectively ceased to be applied in the Western world[30] – as well as to notions of what constituted minimum citizens' rights to welfare and to consideration by the rest of the community. It would be distorting reality to attach a precise date to the onset of this second stage of post-war history. The main point about it was that it was no longer, in any felt sense, 'post-war'. The common underlying trend manifested itself at somewhat different times in different spheres of activity. But the evidence suggests that the change of tempo took effect during the early and middle years of the 1960s, the crucial period being around 1963 to 1968.

In what follows I shall pursue this argument by means of some significant examples, using a broad and selective brush to give shape to the picture. My excuse is that the facts themselves, in addition to the preferences of the author, impose an illustrative rather than a comprehensive approach. The proposition is, after all, not that *all* changed, but that a number of important things did – enough to make a significant difference to the way in which our societies comported themselves. I have already pointed earlier in this chapter to one of the essential ingredients of the process. A ready acceptance of economic change, including socially inconvenient change, when it promised material rewards to those inconvenienced, made the acceleration possible. As the OECD report on the *Interfutures* project put it: 'Structural changes were profound but easily absorbed and growth made it possible to pursue other goals downstream, notably equality and security.'[31]

It should be noticed that there was nothing inevitable about the pursuit of these two particular goals of social policy. Others might have been chosen. However, equality and security were an expression of the spirit of the time. They were rational goals, in view of the fact that mass affluence brought with it additional personal risks. Much of the social history of the West from the early 1960s onwards is concerned with organizing effective forms of public insurance against these risks.

There are at least two different ways in which the beneficiaries of mass affluence grew more vulnerable. One derives from the change in the character of family relationships. As the lives of parents and grandparents lengthened, the traditional obligation on the young and the middle-aged to support their superannuated forebears threatened to become an intolerable burden. The burden was progressively enlarged partly as a simple consequence of the fact that the rate of survival went on rising. At the same time the higher living standards to which people had become accustomed before retirement were much more costly to maintain. Paradoxically, it had been easier to accommodate the old family relationship when the standards of the aged were nearer to subsistence. Expectations rose at the same time as the rest of the family was less able, or willing, to maintain the older members in their accustomed standards of living.

The expectation that basic incomes would not be subject to serious interruptions, whether through age, sickness, or other accidents, was the essentially new demand. It was different from the traditional public insurance schemes which demanded compulsory saving from an early age in order to provide the individual with an *earned* income supplement when circumstances were less favourable. Hugh Heclo and his co-authors, Arnold Heidenheimer and Carolyn Adams, describe the change in the underlying welfare assumptions which occurred during the period up to the 1970s in the following way: 'Entitlement to income security has become less individually earned and more a social right of citizenship.'[32]

The demand for income continuity was related to other, deeper, changes in life styles. Working people were acquiring more and more personal capital goods – homes, household equipment, and vehicles – involving them in the obligation of making regular payments over and above their ordinary current expenditure. Moreover, cars and other equipment are not bought once and for all; they are constantly renewed and replacements are bought on the

basis of long-term contractual arrangements. A parallel principle
applies to many objects that are acquired for use on lease or on a
rental basis. One of the traditional satisfactions of living a middle-
class life is based on confidence about the future, which allows a
buyer or tenant or borrower from a bank to assume long-term
obligations, whose fulfilment depends on having a steady and re-
liable income – the position of the new property-owning working
class is no different. So it is not surprising that once personal affluence came to be taken for granted by a large majority of the
population, there was a demand for measures which would ensure
the constancy of a basic income, in sickness and health, in employment or temporarily out of it, and in the transition to old age.

The politics of welfare in the 1960s and beyond were in large
part a response to this widely felt need. In some versions of the
story, and in particular in the political polemics surrounding it,
public welfare in its post-war guise has been presented as contrasting with vigorous productive effort and the high personal earnings
deriving from it. The enormous importance attached to such welfare, and the very large contributions made to it in taxes on
working-class incomes, in precisely those countries – Germany
being an outstanding instance – where productive effort and wealth
creation have been most successfully achieved, would, it might have
been thought, have prompted a certain prima-facie scepticism about
the argument. In fact the evidence is that the 'new welfare' is widely
conceived of as a natural complement to personal work effort and
high real wages which result from it. The contrast in attitude seems
to be between, on the one hand, the UK and US with their relatively low rates of economic expansion, and, on the other hand,
the extreme welfare societies of central and north-western Europe
where people were getting richer quicker. The significant political
fact to which Heclo again draws attention is that the level of social welfare effort – measured roughly as the proportion of national income devoted to publicly provided social expenditure – is
not in any way correlated with the political position of national
governments.[33] In this matter the difference between self-
proclaimed adherents of the 'right' and the 'left' has clearly been,
at least until the mid-1970s, of minimal importance.

All this suggests that the welfare policy response, reflected in the remarkable increase in the proportion of national output devoted to this purpose, is deeply grounded in the changing character of Western society and that the new commitments which came to be so widely accepted after the Second World War are unlikely to be easily reversed. This is not to say that particular welfare programmes will not be subject to substantial alteration. The point is simply to stress the continuity and vigour with which these collective aims of society were pursued over quite a long period of time. Professor Wilensky has argued that the amount of welfare provision in any given Western society in the 1970s could be predicted by means of three variables: the level of income per capita; the proportion of old people in the population; and, more elusive, the established momentum of the individual social programmes themselves.[34] The last point, which plainly does not lend itself to quantitative measurement, does receive some support from the behaviour of individual countries during the age of acceleration. Between the early 1960s and the mid-1970s total welfare expenditure in the smaller north-west European countries, with a long tradition of public welfare concern, increased with unusual rapidity – much faster than the average of Western countries on the whole. They were led by the Netherlands where welfare expenditure rose to nearly 30 per cent of gross domestic product.[35] By way of extreme contrast, Japan, which traditionally makes modest provision for public welfare, increased the share of GDP devoted to it from 7 per cent to 9 per cent.

By the mid-1970s most of the advanced industrial countries had reached a proportion of 20 per cent or more, the outstanding laggards being the United States and Britain. But the picture of the *rate* of progress by individual countries does not by any means conform consistently with the Wilensky formula. For example the United States, with an especially low public welfare performance at the start of the 1960s, increased the share of its GDP devoted to this purpose by 50 per cent in the course of a dozen years – a significantly faster rate of advance than in Germany or France. These were of course the L. B. Johnson 'Great Society Programme' years. They resulted in a pace of advance that was for a time almost Scandinavian in standard.

For the Western world as a whole some indication of the

magnitude of the advance is given by the (unweighted) average for the OECD countries of the additional share of national resources absorbed by public welfare: it captured an extra share of over 5 per cent of GDP which by the mid-1970s was itself vastly larger than it had been in the early 1970s.[36]

The public welfare drive was the main cause of the marked increase in the share of incomes taken by taxation, again accelerating through the 1960s and early 1970s. The process was universal though far from uniform. Large differences in the tax–take remained; by the early 1970s the American proportion of taxation to national product, the lowest in the North Atlantic area despite the increases of the previous decade, was 40 per cent less than that of the Netherlands and Sweden. One cannot fail to be struck by the very wide variation in what affluent nations regard as a tolerable tax burden. There is also a remarkable constancy about the league table of high, medium, and low tax countries. The first group consists of the smaller industrial countries largely concentrated in north-western Europe; the main members of the second group are Britain, Germany, and France which, for all the differences between them about the appropriate role of government in the economy, converge on a tax ratio of 35–40 per cent of the national product; while the third is an extremely miscellaneous group which includes both the United States and Switzerland.[37]

The OECD's analysis of long-term trends in public expenditure up to the mid-1970s, from which the data that I have cited derive, concluded with a forecast of an imminent change of trend. It argued that after the accelerated advance in welfare provision, the common objective of 'ensuring a basic minimum of income and reasonable access to all the essential services such as education and health' had by the mid-1970s 'largely been achieved' in most of the OECD countries. The prediction seemed plausible and was borne out broadly by subsequent events up to the beginning of 1981. The forecast also points to the qualification that the *full* achievement of basic minima, even in the countries with very well-developed welfare systems, will still involve increased assistance to the poorest groups in society.

Changing Welfare Demands

But there is a deeper question. Even if the forecast turns out to be broadly right in financial terms, does it take sufficient account of the change in the essential content of welfare objectives which accompanied the process of rapid expansion? Aims change as old purposes are accomplished. Social security payments in their traditional form were thought of as providing a minimum of income and of certain essential services to secure a livelihood without degradation during periods when normal earnings were not available. It was an approach based on the conception of the working man as a proletarian, that is a person with no significant assets other than the capacity embodied in his own person to earn his keep. It was assumed that there were no marketable possessions beyond those required for a subsistence living standard – let alone expensive objects which the individual and his family habitually used without having first paid the price of acquiring them. The affluent worker had come to rely upon a flow of services, either bought from outside suppliers or produced, like his television entertainment, by his own equipment at home; and one of the aims of the evolving social policies of the 1960s and 1970s was to ensure that he was not suddenly denuded of these services as a result of circumstances over which he had no control. Accordingly, welfare objectives tended to concentrate more and more on the avoidance of serious disturbance to individual life styles. The latter were generally related to the established income of the individual concerned, and were reflected in turn in the level of his or her statutory contributions to the state social security system. The clearest reflection of this move away from the emphasis on minima was the introduction of differentiated social security compensation for unemployment, old age, etc., based on the previous earnings of the contributor.

This was, in fact, more like the commercial service which a prudent individual would traditionally have tried to buy from a private insurance company. Countries differed in their readiness to respond. In Germany and Sweden, where the ideal of a worker with middle-class standards had infused social welfare philosophy from the start, such demands were more readily accommodated than in those countries in which the basic Anglo-American tradition of a standard minimum required to fend off poverty was the guiding principle. But it is true of Western countries in general, as the authors of *Comparative Public Policy* have observed,[38] that the difference between the principles governing public and private welfare provision through insurance became increasingly blurred. That is not to say that the full-scale insurance principle in public welfare, i.e. the notion that income and outgo in public welfare agencies based on the contributory principle must be kept permanently in balance, was being reinstated – after having been discarded (not without, in some countries, a considerable struggle) as an impediment to the conduct of an effective public policy aimed at raising welfare standards quickly in line with the progress of personal affluence. It was the objective, rather than the means of achieving it, which moved more closely into line with the best commercial practice. Basic rights are established *before* making contributions; but fully paid-up contributors enjoy a wider range of benefits. Old-age pensions are probably the clearest example of the change. There have in fact been three stages in this evolution, as Heclo observes in his study of the struggle over the reform of pensions in Britain and Sweden: '. . . state pensions have been transformed from incidental income supplements to basic subsistence, to wage-related guarantees for living standards.'[39]

Somewhat curiously, the shift of emphasis continued to be justified on the ground of the traditional ideal of equality as the primary objective of civilized society. It is true that to the extent that affluent workers are able to achieve the same types of guarantee of future income standards as those possessed by the well-to-do middle class the inequality between the two classes is reduced. But this is a little remote from the central objective of equality as expressed in the welfare policies of the mid-twentieth century, which were overwhelmingly concentrated on the amelioration of the condition of the most disadvantaged groups. This was where the exponents of the 'new welfare' in the 1960s had come in. The nature of their deviation can perhaps be seen in its sharpest form when it is placed in the context of the guiding philosophy of the earlier approach to welfare, which was given formal expression by John Rawls.[40] I should hasten to say that this was not Rawls's aim: in his view the ethical assumption underlying the key concept of the so-called 'difference principle' was timeless and of universal application. But it happened also to have the virtue – not unknown in the work of other major philosophers of ethics and politics – of giving formal meaning to the sometimes inchoate spirit of contemporary movements of reform. Very briefly put, Rawls's system allows only such inequalities between persons as can be shown positively to assist the primary objective of narrowing the gap between the most disadvantaged group in society and the rest. The ultimate aim is complete equality for everybody. The 'difference principle' provides the guide to appropriate social behaviour *en route* to the ideal.

There is of course much more to Rawls's subtle and intricate approach to political philosophy than this; but for our immediate purpose its relevance is that it provides a coherent version of the principles guiding the liberal social-democratic policies which have been such a powerful force during the post-war period. It is apparent that it has no connection with the 'new welfare' whose basis might be called the 'minimum disturbance principle': its field of reference, while including the most disadvantaged social group, is only incidentally concerned with it. Indeed it is arguable that as the gap between the top, hitherto privileged, ranks of society and the middle layer is reduced by means of the new welfare policies, so the gap between society at large and the most disadvantaged group (which includes many people who are in that group precisely because they are unable to make effective use of the increased facilities for self-help) is likely to be consolidated and reinforced.

It is important, however, to keep the change which is observable with the arrival of mass affluence in perspective. I am not suggesting that the sentiment which is given formal expression in the 'difference principle' ceased to be felt. Concern with the extremely disadvantaged continued to be manifest in certain social reforms. But the characteristic social concerns associated with the age of acceleration, which dates from around the early 1960s, were with such matters as the assertion of women's rights, which began to gather increasing strength at about this time, and with consumers' movements of a predominantly middle-class character, aimed primarily at providing protection against powerful businesses for articulate people equipped with the wherewithal to make substantial purchases of consumer goods. These are in certain ways more akin in spirit to the original nineteenth-century movements which struggled to curb the arbitrary use of authority under the slogan of Liberty, Equality, Fraternity. The equality which the nineteenth-century radicals most eagerly sought was concerned with opportunity. Only later did it acquire its more extensive welfare connotation. My reading of the story is that while this newer connotation dominated the early period after the Second World War, it ceased to supply the leading edge of social policy-making in the second wave of the advance.[41]

In so far as it is possible to measure the practical effects of the explosion of public welfare programmes from the early 1960s onwards, the statistics show that the process still left very large numbers of people in poverty. Surveying the outcome of the great expansion of 'income maintenance programmes' – the most dynamic element in the process – the OECD experts remarked on the disappointing fact that countries which were on average devoting 8–9 per cent of their national product to this purpose were still left with a substantial proportion of the population below the poverty line by the early 1970s.[42] The OECD report pointed out, by way of explanation, that in fact only about one-third of income maintenance expenditures went to the lowest income groups, and commented: 'This is just one aspect of the fact that income maintenance expenditures have not been designed solely, or even primarily, to relieve poverty.'[43] The wider survey of public expenditure trends as a whole, whose results have been referred to earlier, put the point in a somewhat different way which has a direct bearing on the philosophical argument about social and ethical objectives adumbrated above. Summing up the changes in public welfare spending which had occurred up to the early 1970s, it concluded: 'As a very broad generalization . . . it could be suggested that society, over the last decade, has more or less succeeded in fulfilling what might be termed its "democratic" objectives – the extension of coverage to as large a share of the relevant population as possible. Only slow progress, however, has been made towards fulfilling its more "egalitarian" aims involving selective help to the economically vulnerable and socially disadvantaged.'[44]

This account of the aims and outcome of the major advances in welfare spending is worth insisting upon, in view of the arguments which became part of the intellectual stock-in-trade of the late 1970s and beyond, especially in the United States. There was a widely believed legend that the advance had been very largely due to what has been termed an 'explosion of interest groups' operating on a polity too weak to resist them. In the literature which proliferated around this theme, of the State as the feeble defender of the public interest against small but tightly organized groups wanting to put their hands into the public purse, welfare programmes were frequently used as the archetype of the baleful consequences of such pressure-group politics.[45] The facts suggest that they were to a large extent a response to a common anxiety of large numbers of the population seeking more security for themselves and their families, to go with their new-found affluence.

Labour's Response to the Advance in Productivity

We have seen that an essential element in the general process of acceleration which was characteristic of this period was the sharp advance in the rate of increase in labour productivity. It was, of course, also a period of intense labour shortage, especially in Western Europe. Unemployment fell to record low levels in the most successful European economies; in Germany it went as low as 1 per cent and was held at that point, with the exception of one year of recession in 1967, for a decade. European employers engaged in a massive labour recruitment drive outside their own frontiers, and immigration into Western Europe, which had for many years been a labour-exporting region, proceeded on a scale for which there is hardly any precedent – in terms of its effect in changing the composition of the labour force – other than the great waves of migration into the United States before the First World War. By the early 1970s one-tenth of the employed labour force in the two leading European economies, Germany and France, consisted of immigrant workers.

This large shift of population, added to the internal movement of people out of agriculture into more productive occupations, has led some commentators to identify the ready supply of labour for expanding industries as the key to Europe's rapid economic growth.[46] In the specific case of Britain, its relatively slow economic growth, by comparison with that of its neighbours, was seen as being closely connected with the meagre supply of additional labour. Thus Sir John Hicks attributed a large part of the relative lag in British growth rates in the 1950s and 1960s to this fact.[47] Yet the various pieces of the story do not fit easily together. The British case illustrates the problem: in the eleven years up to 1968 UK employment in service trades (on Hicks's classification) rose by 1.6 million,[48] while labour employed in manufacturing declined marginally (by 100,000). Taking the movement into industry and services in total, there was clearly a substantial supply of labour available; it just did not go into jobs in manufacturing. If the European achievement had been mainly due to the shift of workers from relatively low-productivity occupations in agriculture to high-productivity jobs in manufacturing industry, then such facts as these do not readily fit the case. Britain's experience brings out the underlying trend: it was slightly ahead in actually shedding labour from manufacturing industry. This was thought at the time to be exceptional – a special source of weakness in the British economy. But in fact West European industry as a whole absorbed only a modest trickle of additional labour in the late 1960s, and this was followed by an actual decline from 1970 onwards. The main movement of workers was into the 'tertiary sector'. Indeed the employment crisis following the collapse of the boom of 1973 was not the result of a sudden failure of secondary industry to provide jobs, but was above all caused by the 'sharp slowdown in the rate of growth of tertiary sector employment. . . .'[49]

There is something of a paradox here. The sharply rising productivity in manufacturing industry was chiefly responsible for Europe's high rate of growth, but the labour which was so hungrily absorbed was not used where its output would have been highest, but to meet the employment needs of service trades, with their relatively low productivity. It is of course true that some quite significant part of the output of the services sector serves manufacturing industry; [50] transport and communications, retailing and wholesaling are obvious examples. Moreover, productivity in some service activities rose impressively as a result of changes in organization and equipment – like supermarket retailing – during this period. But that does not alter the fact that the momentum of exceptionally rapid economic growth depended mainly on the productivity performance of workers inside manufacturing industry. [51]

What the outcome would have been like if the extra labour taken into employment had not been devoted to meeting the rising demand for services but had gone into manufacturing industry can be seen by looking at Japan; this most dynamic economy of the advanced industrial world illustrates the point vividly. Between 1960 and 1973 Japanese secondary industry absorbed 50 per cent of the very substantial increase in the employed population. This goes a long way towards explaining the overall rise in output per person employed of nearly 9 per cent per year – a rate which was not even approached in Europe or North America. [52]

However, this huge capacity for absorbing workers into secondary industry is not to be regarded as normal, even for Japan. The later years of the 1970s showed that the phenomenon of accelerated growth of the service industries, at the expense of manufacturing, had merely been delayed rather than eliminated. Accordingly, overall Japanese productivity has ceased to rise at quite such a fierce pace as in earlier years. [53]

One conclusion which emerges from this examination of employment trends during the era of high prosperity, when labour was seen as the factor of production which was in especially scarce supply, is that the problem of industrial employment which came to occupy the centre of public attention in the later 1970s was already present at an earlier stage. The established industries were providing fewer and fewer new jobs and, as already noted, during the boom years of the early 1970s were, in Europe, beginning to shed labour. It should have been clear that any significant slackening in the unusually rapid growth of real incomes and, in consequence, of the demand for services on which these incomes were increasingly spent, would quickly convert the erstwhile shortage of labour into a substantial surplus. That productivity should have increased quite so fast at a time when the shake-out of employment in several industries was already being felt, to the extent that it must have been evident to many workers that they were indeed in danger of 'working themselves out of their job' is a noteworthy fact. It reflects a remarkable sense of security which could only be justified by a belief in the ability of the system to maintain in the future the high standard of economic performance, in terms both of jobs and of rising living standards, that it had demonstrated up to that date. The early 1970s were perhaps the climax of post-war confidence, shared by both industrial workers and their employers, in the capacity of the mixed economy to meet their needs.

The consequences of this mood of confidence were not all so favourable to orderly economic progress. Towards the very end of the 1960s, from around 1968 onwards, wage rates in practically all the advanced industrial countries quite suddenly began to rise very sharply indeed, markedly faster than the rise in productivity. The effect over the subsequent period was to double the annual increase in labour costs, compared with the early and middle 1960s.[54] It was a sudden, simultaneous, and unconcerted movement. Very large numbers of people appeared, independently of one another, to have had the same idea. In circumstances like these one naturally looks for a common cause; and a wide variety of explanations have been offered, none of them, however, wholly convincing. Quite probably, there were different motives in different places which prompted the spirit of increased labour militancy.

One element that was almost certainly present has been identified by George Perry in an extensive survey of possible contributing causes.[55] This was the delayed effect of the high profits achieved in the long years of rapidly rising productivity, particularly in the successful economies of Europe and Japan. There came to be a widespread conviction, especially among the leaders of organized labour, that in conditions of such high pressure of demand, so long sustained, it should have been possible, with a little more insistence, to capture a larger share of the revenues accruing to the enterprises in which they worked. Their suspicion then seemed to be amply confirmed by the relative ease with which the employers acceded to much-enlarged wage claims. Thereafter appeals to sweet reasonableness based on the alleged inability of individual firms to pay what was being demanded of them lost their persuasive power. As the exponents of the new militancy saw it, they were, belatedly, only making good their fair share of the winnings which they had previously forgone.

Yet the statistical evidence on the division of earnings between profits and wages lends little support to this view. The share of profits in German and British industry actually declined during the 1960s, and there was no significant change elsewhere, except in Japan. There the ratio of profit went on rising right up to 1973. Elsewhere the effect of the escalation of wage claims starting at the end of the 1960s was to produce a marked shift in the share of national income taken by wages.[56] It is noteworthy and somewhat surprising that this steady gain in labour incomes at the expense of profits did not, at any rate until it reached a very advanced stage, assume the character of a serious confrontation between competing claimants. On the one side was a confident working class bent on increasing its share of the spoils, and on the other a class of employers so anxious to avoid an interruption to the flow of production and earnings that it was ready, at least for a time, to meet the additional demands made on it, with the minimum of resistance. Its members were also, no doubt, confident that they would be able in most cases to offset some of their lost income by putting up prices. The losses, however, outweighed the gains.

The new militancy was a popular movement; its leaders tended to be pushed from behind. Its characteristic instrument was the wildcat strike, or the threat of it, by a body of workers which believed itself to have a particular bargaining advantage, local or professional, that it was determined to exploit whether the official trade union leadership liked it or not. Moderation was at a discount – even in national trade union bodies like those of Germany and Japan with an established and (as later events once again showed) deserved reputation for responsible wage negotiation, taking in wider considerations than the aim of exploiting to the uttermost any immediate bargaining advantage. Indeed the Japanese wage claims of the early 1970s were among the highest conceded in any of the advanced industrial countries. There and elsewhere the inflationary progression of wage claims fed on itself through a generalized process of 'catching up' – first on past claims which were believed to have been forgone, and then on the unexpectedly large gains secured by some more pushful groups of wage-earners, which left the main body of workers determined not to be left behind. Finally, there was the common attempt to catch up on actual and anticipated price increases which were now built into the process itself.

2

The Theory of Nemesis
and the Slowdown
of the 1970s

How far can the acceleration of the 1960s be held to have caused the slowdown of the 1970s? It became fashionable to blame the 'excesses' of the earlier period, etc., etc., for the stubborn difficulties of the later one.[1]

Is it true that the quality of the business cycle following the boom of 1973 would have been different – either in the sense that the trough of the cycle in 1975 would not have been so deep or in the sense that the recovery which followed would have been more rapid or more sustained – if the prosperity of the previous decade and a half had not been pressed quite so hard?

A look at the prima-facie evidence does not immediately lend plausibility to the proposition. Consider the cases of the two countries which can reasonably be held to have pressed their rate of advance in the 1960s to the limit on a wide variety of fronts – Germany and Japan. The Japanese achieved a sustained growth rate up to the early 1970s for which there is no precedent on record. The country's productive capacity was enormously enlarged; vast numbers of workers were drawn into employment, and the number of unemployed was kept below 2 per cent. Neither this nor the fact that demand was constantly pushed to the limits of productive capacity harmed productivity. The high rate

of productivity growth has been discussed in Chapter 1; it rose
faster in Japan than in any other of the OECD countries. It was a
high-risk economy which accepted short-term upsets in its balance
of payments and a higher rate of inflation than other industrial
countries as part of the cost of pursuing long-term national objectives. Then after 1973, following a couple of years of difficulty,
growth was resumed, adding a respectable 5–6 per cent annually
to the national product. This was only just over half of what it
had been previously, but still the best performance of any industrial country. It was accompanied by a relatively low rate of inflation and a balance of payments with a large, indeed embarrass-
ingly large, surplus.

There were of course some aspects of this performance which
were dependent on the special character of Japanese culture and
society. They were characteristic of an exceptionally integrated society, economically backward at the start of the period, which was
intent on exploiting to the full the sudden opportunity for extremely rapid progress. Perhaps therefore the German case, that
of a fully mature industrial society at the start of the 1960s, may
be regarded as more to the point. If there were anything in the
Nemesis theory of economic policy-making, which became so
fashionable in the 1970s – which asserted not only that you cannot eat your cake and have it at the same time, but that you will
also inevitably have indigestion tomorrow – then the German performance would take a lot of explaining. During the 1960s it com-
pressed the rate of unemployment down to levels which had not
previously been regarded as tenable[2] and kept it there for most of
a decade – while national output, which had grown impressively
in the first part of the 1960s, rose, after a brief pause during the
business cycle downturn of 1967, at an even more rapid pace
thereafter. So did the provision of social welfare, both in its volume and range; and so did the balance of payments surplus.

Yet it is hard to find any evidence that, when the break came in
1974, the German economy performed worse than that of other
countries as a result of its earlier excesses. On the contrary, the
relative steadiness of its price level and its very healthy balance of
payments were, in the midst of the oil crisis, more than ever the

envy of the Western industrial world. The achievement was based on an exceptionally good productivity performance – German industrial productivity actually increased faster after 1973 than in the boom years of the early 1970s – and this would not have been possible without the heavy, capital-intensive investment of the period of high prosperity and labour shortage. Industrial employment fell off sharply during the recession; the decline in fact began earlier.[3] Even so, the economy showed remarkable powers of recovery once the opportunity was offered from 1978 onwards, and it ended the decade with the lowest rate of unemployment (3 per cent) of any of the major nations of the North Atlantic area.

Undoubtedly, some of these results were due to good luck as much as to German judgement. Unemployment increased less than elsewhere when jobs were extinguished, because some 800,000 *Gastarbeiter* went home. Secondly, the timing of the German recession of the early 1970s, coming somewhat before the slowdown in other industrial countries, gave Germany's foreign trade an advantage which it was exceptionally well equipped to exploit. The immediate point at issue is whether the German economy suffered any wounds which required special treatment in the late 1970s, because it had for so long been run so close to the limits of its capacity. On the evidence available the answer must be no.

There is a more sophisticated version of the Nemesis theory, which suggests that what made the Western economies so difficult to manage in the second half of the 1970s were essentially the expectations which had been steadily built up by the apparently effortless affluence in the 1960s. As was shown earlier, it was in fact by no means effortless; it involved profound changes in the social framework of the lives of many millions of people. However, all this did occur in an economic context in which the high rate of growth of demand and output made it easy to get new jobs when the old ones disappeared. At the same time the entrepreneurs who took risks, on the basis of the expectation of continued high rates of economic growth, tended to win out. They did not win by any means all the time in all sectors of the economy; but over a long period – during most of a quarter of a century from the late 1940s onwards – the bet on continued economic expansion paid off. As was observed earlier, instead of slowing down, as many had expected at the end of the 1950s, the pace speeded up further right into the 1970s.

Can the blame for the inadequate performance which followed the great boom of the early 1970s be fairly placed on an ironclad confidence about the future derived from the very long experience of almost continuous prosperity? It became a commonplace of the period of the economic slowdown that expectations whose source lay in the earlier experience had placed a great weight on Western society, making it altogether less agile and responsive, and that the aim of economic policy must be to change them. The latter objective applied most especially to inflationary expectations – though on the basis of historical evidence such expectations tend on the whole to stimulate the borrowing entrepreneur, who invests in real assets today in the hope of paying back his debt cheaply, out of sales of higher-priced products derived from his investment, in the future. However, there was another expectation to contend with – of a slowdown in the rate of economic growth, compared with the recent past – which made investment in productive assets appear more risky and doubtful. Some economists argued that the latter view, which held back the growth of productive investment during the 1970s in most countries of the Western world, also derived from the first. The expectation of continued inflation, it was suggested, led businessmen to believe that sooner or later governments would impose sharp deflationary measures on the economy, with a consequent steep fall in business activity.

Whether this was an accurate account of business psychology has not been proved. The important point was that a number of factors combined to curb business investment and to slow down the advance of economic activity, while prices continued to rise during the second half of the 1970s at a sustained pace which had not been seen before in a period of reduced growth and higher unemployment during this century. The unusual combination of low economic activity with sharply rising prices plainly could not have been sustained if the traditional 'clearing mechanism' of markets had been functioning properly, i.e. if prices had consistently adjusted to the point where demand and supply were brought into balance. Least of all did this apply to the market for labour. Organized labour had established its own arrangements between the wars to put a floor under wage earnings; now these arrangements were buttressed by public institutions which set unemployment pay at a much higher proportion of average wages than in the past. The proportion had risen progressively in the previous thirty years, and it varied from country to country, ranging typically (for the initial period of unemployment) from about two-thirds to nine-tenths of previous earnings.[4] A high minimum wage was therefore the starting point for bargaining about real wage claims between employers and workers. Then labour's expectations about the rate of inflation in the period ahead made pay claims rise still higher, and to the extent that they were met, inflationary expectations were in large part self-validating. Thus on neither side, apparently, were the dominant expectations about prices and about future economic activity based on the long experience *preceding* the early 1970s; the decisive factor would have to be the much shorter experience in the more recent past.

It might be argued, however, that the underlying attitudes on the side of labour – the assumption that high wage claims could be met without adverse effects on the level of employment – were greatly influenced by the long record of success following the Second World War, which culminated in the accelerated economic and social advance of the late 1960s. Neither labour nor capital – in this respect they shared the same attitude – seriously believed in the probability of a deep slump. The brief drop in production which occurred throughout the Western world in 1975 – the first such universal decline experienced for more than a quarter of a century – was, after all, no more than a minor economic reverse by the standards of the past. Those standards had their origin in that, as Arthur Lewis has pointed out, during the seventy years from 1870 until 1940, 'no decade would pass without a great depression in one or other of the four leading industrial countries'.[5] And that experience, as he observes, had a profound effect on people's attitudes towards the economic system on which they depended for their livelihood. Uncertainty became the rule. Over the whole period it produced a shock effect 'which the free market ideology could not possibly survive, except in isolated ideological

enclaves'.[6] By contrast, from the late 1940s onwards the experience of economic catastrophe was absent; after the war social welfare and successful capitalist enterprise advanced together; there
was no persuasive evidence that the two were not indissolubly
bound up with each other.

The Unconvincing Depression

It could be argued on this reading of economic behaviour that the
short shallow recession of 1975 was especially damaging in its
long-term effects – more damaging than a thoroughgoing slump.
It was a recession which was significant enough to change investment behaviour, and thus to reduce the future capacity for economic growth, but was not on a sufficient scale to alter the expectations of wage-earners about the rate of increase in living
standards. It was an unusual business collapse in the course of
which wage-earners managed, in spite of rising unemployment, to
increase their share of the national income at the expense of profits. A depression of the familiar historical type, the commonplace
of the century before the Second World War, would have changed
all that. It is hardly conceivable that the basis of wage bargaining
would *not* have been affected by a changed sense of the risk to
both parties of an agreement which caused a sharp rise in prices.
It is not that the awareness of such a risk was now entirely absent.
But it had been attenuated by the effects of the extensive apparatus of the welfare state, and more generally by the acceptance
of ultimate government responsibility for the successful functioning of the mixed economy established throughout most of the
Western world since the Second World War.

Yet the story of the 1975 economic crisis which was not allowed to become a depression is not the simple tale of a rescue
operation in which governments provided aid and comfort to a
mixed economy in trouble. The role of many governments and of
the public agencies, like central banks, associated with them, was,
as their subsequent behaviour showed, more equivocal. They were
in general – though there were some exceptions – determined to
limit the business of pump-priming the economy to the bare minimum; their dominant anxiety was to avoid anything which might

be held to give encouragement to those whose unshaken confidence in the early return of a low-risk (or no-risk) economy helped to sustain inflationary expectations. They wanted these expectations to be shaken up, to demonstrate unmistakably that prices could fall in response to falling demand and that it was not a sensible policy, either for businessmen or for trade unionists, to bet on unending growth with inflation.

There was in fact a remarkable unison about the responses of the leading industrial countries of the West to the shock of 1974/5. The stimulus of demand from the public sector, i.e. the extent to which government buying from the rest of the economy exceeded the money that it extracted in taxes, everywhere increased.[7] Where this increased relatively little between 1974 and 1975, as in the UK, it was because the main stimulus of enlarged deficit spending had been applied in 1974, at an earlier stage in the business downturn.

However, there were some interesting differences in tactics and timing. Real public expenditure in some of the major countries rose only moderately – in the UK and Germany by less than the increase registered earlier during the peak year of the boom in 1973. In fact, the main economic stimulus, through the fall in taxes, came in large part as an automatic result of lower income from employment and sharply reduced profits caused by the recession. The outcome was that the mass of disposable income rose in real terms in all the major countries, as their production fell off. The built-in stabilizers of these economies, which had been gradually put in place over the previous fifteen years, worked. It required no hurried decisions by governments to ensure that, during the first onset of a slump, output and personal incomes moved in opposite directions. Private consumption accordingly went up at a time when the drop in business confidence and activity depressed output and reduced employment.[8]

But after the great year of the economic stabilizers the pattern of behaviour changed. The Bank for International Settlements in its annual report for 1977/8 noted that, whether 'by deliberate choice or because of unforeseen developments, fiscal policy in many countries became more restrictive in late 1976 and for much of 1977'. The change of trend reflected a more profound sentiment

which the BIS described as 'a growing conservatism in the use of
discretionary fiscal policy for economic management'.[9] The sentiment, however, took hold in different countries to a very different
degree. The United States, which was barely affected by it, and
Japan were both able to move on from the upturn in 1976 to a
consolidation of their economic recovery. In the United States the
movement developed rapidly into a full-scale boom with a strong
advance in industrial investment. The process was aided by a
series of tax breaks from 1977 onwards – coincident with the
arrival of the Carter Administration which had gained its election
victory at the end of 1976 on the promise of a policy of high
employment and sustained economic expansion.

In Japan, too, the rate of growth did not falter; it was above
the best performance of the other OECD countries, even though
it did not return to the exceptional Japanese tempo of the 1960s
and early 1970s. The economic impulse which supported the expansion owed a great deal to the sustained and greatly enlarged
budget deficit, more than double the 1973/4 average; public
spending here took the form of selective investment subsidies, deliberately aimed at making good the missing capital inputs from
the private sector. The Japanese government took the radical step
of breaking through the strict limit previously imposed on deficit
financing (30 per cent of the budget) in the process.

It was in Western Europe that the reversal of policy during the
very early stages of the 1976 recovery was most keenly felt. Almost as soon as the first signs of economic revival began to appear
government expenditure was curbed, while at the same time disposable personal incomes were squeezed as taxation rose. The latter phenomenon was less a deliberate policy decision than a consequence of rising incomes and prices. As real wages rose nominal
wages rose even faster, and that increased the proportion of total
earnings falling into the fiscal net through progressive income taxation.

Here were the automatic stabilizers, which had served so well
in 1975, operating in reverse – and doing so with a vengeance.
Changes in net taxation (including transfer payments by the state
for welfare and other purposes), whose combined effect in the seven
large OECD countries had been to increase total real personal income by nearly 3 per cent in 1975, reduced it by around 1 per

cent in the following year; and there was a further reduction in 1977.[10] When an incipient economic recovery is as delicately poised as it was in 1976, a switch in public finance whose net effect was to cut back the rate of growth of spendable personal incomes by 3 per cent from one year to the next may easily be decisive (though it is impossible to measure its precise effect on the actual outcome). The year 1976 was also one in which real wage earnings rose strongly as production recovered. There was a marked improvement in productivity too – against the general trend of the second half of the 1970s. It may be that the sharp upturn in 1976 would in any case have flattened out later; but the subtraction from personal incomes caused by the fiscal turn-round made certain that it did, speedily and effectively.

The Commission of the European Communities (CEC), in a retrospective survey of 'Economic Cycles in the 1970s', concluded categorically that in Europe the 'economic policy stance contributed to the premature slowing-up of the recovery process'.[11] Perhaps a more remarkable aspect of European behaviour was that the 'contractionary budgetary policy' was persisted in, despite the clear evidence of feeble consumer demand and even feebler private sector investment: 'After the recovery process had weakened in the latter half of 1976 policy-makers continued to be constrained by high budget deficits, inflationary pressures and, in some countries, weak currencies, to maintain at best an overall neutral posture.'[12] That is another way of saying that active demand management policies of a Keynesian type were, after a brief interlude in 1975, not applied. The 'neutral posture' of governments referred to by the European Commission included in practice some instances in which the growth of public expenditure was sharply cut back; and almost everywhere central banks put a squeeze on the supply of money. The worry about inflation overrode other considerations. It was combined with what seems in retrospect an extraordinary confidence on the part of those responsible for the policy of demand restraint in the boundless capacity of the economies under their supervision to regain of their own accord the absent momentum of vigorous growth. It was as if governments were overcome by an irresistible impulse to shout, like a boastful bicycle rider: 'Look, no hands!'

There were exceptions: the United States has already been

mentioned. In addition to the largest of the advanced industrial countries, a number of the smaller nations of Western Europe persisted in the view that, when economic activity was sluggish because demand was slack, the proper response was for governments to use the ample powers at their disposal to raise the level of demand and output. But such ideas ran counter to the dominant line of thinking in Western Europe. The fashionable talk at the time was about structural factors, particularly on the 'supply side' of the economy, which presented problems that no amount of pump-priming of demand could possibly remedy.[13] Capital, it was argued, failed to respond to opportunities for investment regardless of the financial incentives offered, and on the other side labour of the type required was not forthcoming in the places where it was in demand. People in general were saving more while businessmen were investing less. The moral to be drawn seemed to be that there was precious little that governments *could* do – except, possibly, to improve labour-market information for job-seekers and potential employers and to supply additional training for workers to overcome the temporary 'mismatch' between supply and demand.

That there should be plenty of savings concurrently with a low level of investment and that it should prove difficult to induce business to employ more labour was a situation that was by no means unfamiliar to Western capitalism. It was where Keynes came in in the 1930s. It was no part of the lesson that was learnt then that the remedy was easy; it might well take time and a lot of stubborn effort to change the expectations of businessmen and others through public intervention. It was, rather, the experience of the quarter of a century after the Second World War which had established the assumption that it was going to be quick and painless – and that if it wasn't, the method did not work. Perhaps, after all, it was government expectations, rather than those of business and labour, which had been most profoundly influenced by the long experience of sustained economic growth.

This is not to deny that there were strange and unexpected features of the economic slowdown – notably the association of large-scale unemployment and poor business with continuing high inflation. It was enough to make governments wary. It took time and a great deal of international effort to persuade them that something more needed to be done than to go on standing on the sidelines talking gloomily about problems of 'supply side economics'. It required, nevertheless, a good deal of persuasion to bring about the change of policy, with the focus on demand management, which was formally agreed in mid-1978 at a summit meeting of the heads of the main Western governments in Germany. The Germans were in fact by this time the key factor in the international economy, together with the Japanese. The two nations had emerged rapidly and successfully from the balance of payments problems, brought on by the first oil crisis of the 1970s, and had then moved into massive current account surplus. But whereas Japan also moved to a higher rate of growth, and held it after 1976, Germany did not. Another point of difference was that Japan's most important trading partner was the United States which had more than once shown that it possessed the ability in the last resort to persuade Japanese policy-makers to take full account of American economic interests; Germany's main trading partners, on the other hand, were the other countries of the European Community, which possessed much less collective clout when it came to an argument about the need to adapt German domestic policy to the needs of outsiders.

An International Planned Recovery, 1979/80

Nevertheless, it was the EEC, at a summit meeting of its political leaders, that provided the occasion for the first clear signal that a change of course in economic policy was now overdue.[14] The formalities of international pressure were not unimportant in this instance. It may be argued that it would in any case have proved impossible, and that this was already becoming clear to the Germans, for them to maintain a relatively prosperous economy relying for its main stimulus on international trade, while other countries hesitated to lift the level of their economic activity because of deficits which were, in some measure, the counterpart of German surpluses. But at the level of overt public statement, at least, the Germans seemed pretty tenacious in their attachment to their existing policies. It was indeed a novel and difficult task to determine by international agreement the differences in the amount and kind of stimulus which it was proper to ask individual countries (under different degrees of constraint) to apply to their own economies. Possibly in consequence, an extraordinary amount of effort went into the selection of the right words to cover the deed. The Germans particularly objected to the original proposals which were couched in terms of the 'locomotive principle', i.e. that a leading country should provide the initial impulse for the economic advance and then pull the others along behind it. It was offensive because it might be held to imply that someone with a powerful engine that was ready and available for use was deliberately keeping it idle in a railway siding. The image was no more popular with the Japanese, who were also expected to provide part of the extra pulling power for the rest of the world economy.

An alternative verbal invention – 'the convoy principle' – which politely suggested leadership at the head of a line of vehicles rather than actual pulling power, did hardly any better. In the end the Western leaders contented themselves with the pallid formula, invented by the OECD, of a 'programme of concerted action' – acceptable because it implied clearly that everyone had responsibilities which were not in principle different in degree, even though some might have a greater capacity than others to carry them. Once the Germans had been persuaded to accept what they then termed their 'international obligations',[15] they moved in a massive way into the deficit financing of economic expansion. It was a carefully designed programme, choosing among the alternative means available those which were likely to produce a major boost to the momentum of the economy at large with the greatest speed. Public investment plans were, to use the current jargon, 'front-loaded'. A sudden flood of orders for projects in the public sector, or ancillary to it, were to give a lift to investment, while higher personal incomes deriving from a series of cuts in direct taxation were to stimulate consumer expenditure.

The German authorities pursued the new policy with the energy and verve characteristic of recent converts to a cause. The cause was to mobilize every possible means available to the government to induce German industrial investment to resume the advance which had made Germany the world's leading exporter of manufactured goods in the 1960s. Even before the big public investment programme was translated into a flow of orders to German firms, the announcement effect of the well-advertised change of course made itself felt. The economic advance in the second half of 1978 accelerated into the beginnings of a boom in the following year.

It is worth noting that the whole operation was designed in such a way as to establish full confidence among the business community in the government's commitment to the new approach and, most particularly, in the durable character of the decisions that had been taken. A deliberate effort was made to convince businessmen that the authorities had firmly committed themselves to a programme of public expenditure, spread over a number of years, which would ensure a continuing high rate of growth of output. This involved a rather different and more complex approach to the process of demand management than the traditional versions of the process, with their overwhelming emphasis on the short-term. As the German Council of Economic Experts pointed out in its 1978 Annual Report, the stimulus to investment demand would be effective only if the business community were assured that the fiscal boost was *not* a once-and-for-all operation. To this end the government's medium term *Finanzplan* (covering a four-year period up to 1982) had to be radically adapted to allow for a larger annual budget deficit in the early 1980s.[16] Without this, even assuming that the typical investment project involved a lead time of as little as two or three years, the incentive would not work. There was the further implication that the attempt at persuasion would not be effective if it relied simply on broad promises of future government action: the assurance of continuing public intervention sufficient to sustain growth would become credible only if it were seen to be an integral part of the logic of official thinking about the longer-term requirements of the German economy. That is what the amended *Finanzplan* set out to provide. It argued that, on the basis of the best forecast that the authorities were able to make, the achievement of a high rate of German economic growth over the years ahead required that the normal expansion of demand from private sources be systematically supplemented by a larger than normal increase in public spending. That implied substantial budget deficits, larger than in the past, in each year up to and including 1982; and the Ministry of Finance proceeded to work out a programme of increased public borrowing on that assumption.

This aspect of the German decision of 1978, made under intense international pressure, is worth recounting in detail for two reasons. First, like the Japanese decision (taken in parallel with the German) to add further to the already growing volume of public investment, it required an explicit change in a major aspect of policy to which the government and the powerful bureaucracies (including the central banks) in the two countries had attached themselves. In the Japanese case it was the rigid ceiling hitherto fixed on the size of the budget deficit that had to be broken through.[17] In Germany it was a major alteration in the character of the *Finanzplan* whose official function is to provide the guidelines for the behaviour of ministries and other public agencies. The earlier doctrine had been that public finance should be a 'neutral' factor in the development of the economy, neither furthering nor retarding the pace of growth determined by other causes; now it was converted into an active producer of deficits designed to stimulate a higher rate of growth than would otherwise have been achieved.[18]

The second point of interest is that the obligation which the German authorities undertook in amending the *Finanzplan* was, at least in its intention, of the same kind as that of a French government when it commits itself to one of its series of National Plans. The analogy between the two has become especially close as the process of French planning has moved away from coordinated target-setting for all industries and branches of production to a programme centred on the effects of a series of key inputs from the public sector into the economy. This change of emphasis was clearly spelt out for the first time in the VIIth Plan, 1976–80, and figured largely in the great debate of the early 1970s about the essential character of economic planning in conditions of increasing business uncertainty.

There are of course other aspects of French planning which go beyond what may be termed the *Finanzplan* approach – that is, steering the economy by means of medium-term budgetary promises. The point that is worth making, however, is that the degree of convergence in the essential methods of economic policy-making was, and is, greater than French politicians and their audiences or, for that matter, their German counterparts, think.[19] This is not so much a case of mass deception by élites who know but will not tell, as of the élites being deceived by their attachment to their stereotypes of themselves and of their neighbours and to the established styles of rhetoric which serve to exaggerate the differences between them.

By the late 1970s Germany had become a force in the making of international economic policy to a degree which it had never been before – whether at the height of imperial power before the First World War or during the period of 'peaceful invasion' of Central and Eastern Europe preceding the Second. The situation was essentially different because the Federal Republic of Germany, though reduced in size and population – possibly *because* it had been so reduced – had converted itself into a much more open economy. Its exports, which now absorbed about one-quarter of its national product and close to one-half of its output of manufactured goods,[20] were spread widely across the world, though with a strong emphasis on Western Europe. There, a number of countries were so closely tied into the German market that even quite small changes in German domestic policy could broaden or narrow their room for manoeuvre in a decisive way.

To some extent the establishment of the European 'Monetary Snake'[21] was a simple recognition of this fact. The group of small countries in this D-Mark zone, several of whom were dependent on the German market for around 30 per cent of their external trade, could not in fact afford to move far out of line with German economic and monetary policy without grave risk to the solvency of their economies. In these circumstances, it seemed a sensible idea to advertise the fact that one was bound in this way, and thus perhaps acquire some more international confidence in the stability of one's currency and good financial behaviour. Germany itself had become dependent on these small countries, too – as much as 25 per cent of its exports were sold to the member countries of the reduced 'Snake'. But in terms of the constraints which the latter were able to impose on German policy-making, the relationship was very different. The same was true in practice even for France, Germany's biggest single trading partner. Mutual dependence does mean something different when one of the partners to the relationship is notably larger, in terms of economic mass, and is believed, quite plausibly in this case, to have more economic options open to it than the other. It was France which waited on the shift in German economic policy to a more expansionist stance in the late 1970s, not the other way about.

Yet it would be misleading to think of the marked change in European policy-making at the latter end of the 1970s in terms of a picture of Germany with a starting-pistol telling the others when to go. There was a genuine and widespread change of mood following the failure of the first attempt – after the slump of the mid-seventies – to get back to earlier high levels of economic growth. Keynesian-type measures of demand management, which had been dismissed as outmoded and irrelevant, enjoyed a certain revival on the Continent of Europe (though not in Britain, where they were treated with especially dismissive contempt by the Conservative Government of Mrs Thatcher which came into office in 1979). If such moves had initially a tentative quality, it was at least in part because German official rhetoric, which had something of the quality of the confident exposition of the only true faith, had caused inhibitions, especially as we saw earlier in the conduct of the international debate on policy. Once the decision to embark on the programme of 'concerted action' had been formally taken at the summit meeting of the leaders of the seven major industrial nations of the West in Bonn in the summer of 1978, Germany's vigorous response to it gave confidence and momentum to a process that was already – though hesitantly – beginning to get under way.

Moreover, it looked as if the next phase of economic expansion at the international level was going to be admirably *desynchronized* – with Germany and Japan speeding up the tempo while the United States slowed down. After the earlier fumbling, this seemed to be a model of international co-ordination. In the view of the OECD, which had itself been largely instrumental in formulating this programme, its rapid effects had by 1979 changed 'the geographical pattern of the demand expansion' on a global scale.[22] The clearest demonstration that the international economic balance really was shifting was the precipitate drop in the value of the Japanese yen against the dollar, losing in less than a year one-third of its value compared with the peak rate of exchange reached towards the end of 1978.

However, in the end the smooth conversion of economic laggards into leaders and vice versa, which had been hoped for, did not quite work. This piece of 'fine tuning' was in any case going to be a hazardous business. The laggards, notably the Germans, had waited too long before they took action. Since Germany so largely influenced the economic pace in Western Europe as a whole, the result was to impose a particular strain on the United States which was left to conduct a solitary economic advance in an unfavourable international environment. Equally, the United States was very slow to convince itself that its large balance of payments deficit, which reached record proportions as its economic boom went forward in the second half of the 1970s, had to be taken seriously – that is, seriously enough to be treated as a limiting factor in the conduct of its own domestic policy. It was almost a point of principle for members of the original Carter Administration that the balance of payments of a great country like the United States should be left to look after itself – that it was unworthy to allow temporary increases in the current account deficit to determine government policies either on important domestic issues, like employment, or on international matters, where the United States was engaged in exercising its functions of political and economic leadership in the non-Communist world.

It was a heroic doctrine to pursue at a time when the position of the dollar as an international reserve currency had greatly weakened compared with the 1960s. The US had in fact lost its commanding position in world capital markets, at the same time as the movement of international capital had vastly increased in scale and in its influence on economic development. The great accumulation of dollar balances by the Middle East countries following the 350 per cent oil price rise in 1973/4 seemed for a time to have given the dollar respite from the international pressures that had been growing over the years. But as the American economy expanded, against the economic trend in the rest of the world, the crisis of confidence re-emerged in an acute form. With some 80 per cent of the world's currency reserves held in dollars, even a modest move to diversify these holdings, as a matter of prudent investment policy, by selling off a portion of the dollar assets could, and did, have drastic effects on the day-to-day price of the currency in foreign exchange markets. Moreover, such a fall in the exchange parity of a currency in widespread use for all manner of private transactions tends to be cumulative. A little diversification by everyone then becomes indistinguishable from an irresistible speculative attack on the currency concerned.

This is what happened just at the time when the OECD's 'international concerted action' was in process of altering the international balance of trade in America's favour. It coincided, too, with the second major increase in the price of oil by the OPEC countries in 1979. It was not that this had a more serious economic effect on the United States than on other industrialized countries. Almost all of them moved into deficit on their current balance of payments. The difference for the United States was that the setback occurred precisely at the moment when the gradual improvement in its external position was about to show up in a dramatic shift from a long-standing current account deficit into a visible and substantial surplus. The Americans needed this visible demonstration in order to provide relief to their capital account, increasingly hard pressed as foreign governments and businesses sold dollars in order to acquire other monetary assets which looked as if they might be more stable in value. One aspect of the investor's view of what constituted a stable currency, which American policymakers had certainly underestimated, was the belief that it belonged to a nation which demonstrated that it was able consistently to earn enough foreign exchange to cover its current needs.

This combination of accidents goes a long way towards explaining why the Western world was once again baulked of a general and sustained economic recovery at the start of the 1980s. The stage was set for such an event, and the conduct of demand management in the key countries was, after some earlier mistakes, well designed to secure the desired outcome. Subsequent legend may tell the story differently, to demonstrate that the capacity of expansive demand management in contemporary conditions proved once again too feeble to produce more than transient results.[23] In fact it was not seriously tried out until very late; and then the experience was prematurely cut short by external events.

Critique: the Hayek and Friedman Versions

It might, however, be argued that to regard these happenings as 'external' to the main scene is to beg the essential question. Might it not, after all, be that they were, in spite of appearances, endogenous to the mixed economy – a natural outcome of the way that the latter was being run with a high degree of public intervention which consistently frustrated or weakened market forces? A severe version of this kind of critique, of which Hayek has been perhaps the most notable spokesman, asserts that because of the measures which cushioned the effects of economic fluctuations on employment and wages, structural adjustments – required to adapt production to demand – were avoided and in consequence unemployment in the long run is higher than it otherwise would have been. Short-term pump-priming, in other words, has aggravated the underlying problem, not eased it. At the same time, the manner in which soft fiscal and monetary policies weakened the discipline of the market on wage-earners encouraged the latter to make inflationary wage claims and gave employers an incentive to adapt to them. (Under the heading of the soft fiscal approach would be included the various welfare measures referred to in Chapter 1, which in combination have the effect of artificially lifting the minimum wage and, it is alleged, reinforcing workers' resistance to change – thus inflating the real cost of labour per unit of output.)

Professor Hayek was also the exponent of the remedy of the short sharp shock for the ills of the 1970s – a non-gradual reduction of the growth of money. The shock, on his prescription, would have to be sharp enough not only to cause a much larger increase in the number of unemployed but also to make their condition much less comfortable – in order to alter the trade-off between having a job (under the new flexible conditions of work) and being without one. Yet in contrast to the remarkably similar remedy he had proposed more than forty years before, in the depths of the great depression of the 1930s (and, one might add, in apparent contrast to some of his professed followers), he is now sufficiently aware of the 'downward rigidity of money wages' in the short term to limit the reduction of the money supply to a level where it does not cause 'real' or 'secondary deflation', i.e. push the economy into a depression.[24]

It should be observed that this approach to the problem was very different from that of the straightforward 'monetarist' policies which secured wide and increasing support during the 1970s – although in practice the two schools seemed to be content to present themselves as natural partners in a coalition against Keynesians who were in their view over-eager and over-confident in their pursuit of short-term objectives. But this was solely a tactical coalition against a common enemy. It was no part of the monetarist philosophy to require the application of violent shocks to the economy. Indeed, the leading exponent of this approach, Professor Milton Friedman, constantly emphasized the need to allow time for the consistent application of a monetary policy, that was decreasingly accommodating to rises in wages and other costs, to have its full effect. This effect would depend in the end on altering *expectations* in such a way as to change the terms of wage and price bargaining. The authorities accordingly needed the demonstration effect of a policy of refusal, consistently pursued, in order to persuade these bargainers to change their style. Increased unemployment resulting from the squeeze on the money supply would of course be one of the means of persuasion. But it was not regarded as being necessary in itself to induce reluctant workers to accept more profound changes of the kind which adherents of the Hayek school held to be necessary to achieve long-term high employment. Indeed, the monetarists took the view that policies which attempted to stimulate economic activity beyond the level set by the 'natural rate of employment' could not have more than temporary and barely significant effects on the real economy. Such policies could not in the long run affect the volume of production, but only the prices that people had to pay for what was produced.

This led to a comparatively modest version of the economics of Nemesis – that profligate monetary policies, when persisted in, made the process of adjusting to a non-inflationary cost structure take longer. There is little doubt that as a general proposition this is true, and also that an unusually large number of different countries in the early 1970s were notably lax in exercising control over the growth of the national money supply. The boom of 1973 was, partly in consequence of this, exceptionally inflationary by previous post-war standards. There were other contingent circumstances which derived from causes that were not man-made, notably the steep rise in food prices caused by the disastrous harvests of that year. But the peculiar staying power of inflation during the economic downturn which followed surely owed something to the vast stock of extra money which had been introduced into the system earlier. Where the monetarist analysis is less satisfactory is in the spirit of exclusiveness which seems to be inherent in it. At any rate, its practitioners appear to be subject to an irresistible urge to assert, in a style reminiscent of more ancient doctrines: 'Money supply is great, and there is no force other than the money supply.'

Japanese Remedies

As a guide to policy, this has the effect of seriously underestimating the influence of different institutional capacities in advanced industrial societies. It accordingly tends to distort the varied picture of the performance of the industrial world during the testing time of the 1970s and after. Consider the experience of Japan. It was outstandingly the most successful of all the industrial countries in reversing a dizzy increase in the rate of inflation during the final stages of the boom of the early 1970s, and doing so faster than anyone else. Wholesale prices rose by 31 per cent in 1974 and then by only 3 per cent in 1975. That is the extreme case. If the field is extended to include such items as public services (where cost per unit rose by 14 per cent between 1974 and 1975), the drop shown in the rate of increase of consumer prices as a whole between the two years was from 24.5 per cent to just under 12 per cent.[25] During the same period the annual increase in wage earnings fell from 27 per cent to just under 15 per cent – and then went on steadily falling, so that the rate of increase was halved again by 1978. Now the crucial factor in this was the concerted action to curb a wide range of price increases, at the expense of lower profits and increased subsidies, during 1975. That was a necessary condition for the sudden outburst of wage moderation which reversed the trend of previous years.

The story of how Japanese incomes policy worked in the mid-1970s to achieve the sudden break in previous trends is a complicated one, and a brief account cannot do full justice to it. The absence of alternative job opportunities was a factor (here as elsewhere), though the direct impact of the slump on unemployment levels was *less* here than in other countries. The level of registered unemployment never rose much above 2 per cent, largely as a result of discriminating dismissals which concentrated on people at or just above the age of retirement and on young girls who went back to their families and ceased to look for employment. But large numbers of redundant workers were retained, on the basis of well-established understandings about security of employment – a factor which explains both the precipitous drop in productivity which occurred during 1975 and the even more drastic reduction in profits. Many firms were in fact running at a loss, disguised commonly in company annual reports by the sale of corporate capital assets and their conversion in the accounts into current income. Unit labour costs in manufacturing rose by 17 per cent, while prices at retail and wholesale level increased by less than half that amount.

These were some of the elements of the high-risk strategy adopted by Japanese business and government in pursuit of an incomes policy which would bring down the level of wage settlements. It was remarkably successful, though not in its immediate impact – unit wage costs continued to rise very sharply in 1975 – but over the longer term. In fact, the combination of the continued fall in wage earnings in 1976, with the massive increase in manufacturing productivity (14 per cent in one year) as business revived, brought the increase in unit labour costs down almost to zero. It is of course quite clear that this remarkable turnaround could not have been achieved without a process of wage bargaining which was peculiarly successful in making wage-earners sensitive to the rise and fall in the fortunes of the enterprises which employ them. In particular the regular payment of half-yearly bonuses, which vary in amount and rise to as much as a quarter .or more of total earnings in a good year, has the effect of linking earnings directly with profits. Effectively, employees take on something of the character of involuntary shareholders in the businesses in which they work. At the same time, however, Japanese trade unions are not weak – about one-third of the labour force is unionized – and the leadership (in addition to persuading its own members) has to be persuaded that wage moderation in a difficult time is being matched by a serious effort on the part of management to limit the loss of jobs and to hold down prices. This is the essential bargain underlying any incomes policy. In Japan it was systematically supported by the government which had the power to control the prices of important commodities with a high degree of popular prominence (e.g. oil prices), and used it. It also took measures to support business activity in a number of ways which involved a very substantial rise in public expenditure.[26]

Incomes Policies and 'Customer Markets'

This Japanese endeavour to use public power and finance, in concert with business, to hold prices below the level that they would have reached under the exclusive dominance of market forces, and to sustain employment above it, has been described in some detail because it provides a striking illustration of the extent to which incomes policies can be effective as a means of steering the economy. There is no support here for the view that such efforts are of their nature ephemeral and are fairly promptly offset by an equal and opposite movement which is bound to undo the temporary good work in the longer term. Other illustrations, from other countries, are available; but it would require more elaborate analysis of the detail to make the same point. Japan will do: it is after all the second largest economy in the non-communist world. It has also had, fairly consistently, the highest growth rate since the Second World War. The monetarist position is that incomes policies of this character can *never* be effective. Indeed the argument goes further; according to the authors of a wide-ranging monetarist survey of such efforts throughout the ages, from the Emperor Diocletian to Britain under Harold Wilson, '. . . the cost

of most of the measures usually known as "incomes policy"
far exceeds the benefits. . . .'[27] In this case, in contrast to the vain
attempts to use fiscal or monetary means to raise economic activity above the level set by the 'natural rate of employment', the
monetarists take the view that real damage may well be done to
the economy. This is because trade unions, as part of the price of
agreeing to policies of wage moderation, invariably demand of the
public authorities that they take measures which will artificially
hold down prices. And this, it is alleged, inevitably distorts market
forces governing the relative costs of different goods and services
in such a way as to mess up the crucial decisions of entrepreneurs
which determine a nation's capacity to produce wealth.

There is a large literature of debate on the effects of incomes
policies in recent times.[28] It usually proceeds by one side showing
that the price and wage norms promulgated by governments are
invariably breached. The other side counters by demonstrating that
incomes policies, if flexibly and intelligently conducted, can be
shown on certain assumptions about the earlier trend to have had
some effect in reducing prices marginally below the level that they
would have reached if there had been no interference with the
market process.[29] Apart from the difficulties of such hypothetical
types of measurement, there is the key problem, already mentioned, of deciding on the appropriate time-span for an analysis
of the effects. The practice in this country is to judge specific incomes policies (whether British or foreign) on the basis of the statistical evidence of a trend within the time-scale of a single business cycle, that is about five years or so. Whereas the Japanese
effort works on this time-scale, the incomes policies of other countries do not – notably the British experiment, which achieved some
marked success for a short period in 1976 in holding down wages,
a success that was, however, fully offset by higher wage increases
in subsequent years. For our present purpose the demonstration
that such policies of intervention are *sometimes* feasible and, in a
limited way, effective is sufficient: it tells one something about the
scope for the possible use of public power in a modern mixed
economy.

This is not to argue that exhortation can hold down wages and
prices indefinitely, in the face of fiscal and monetary policies mak-

ing for inflation. That proposition provides the material for the straw man which polemicists have spent so much time knocking down. Nor is the typically successful version of a sustained incomes policy usually characterized by an officially promulgated percentage norm to which everyone, regardless of different circumstances, is supposed to adhere. That kind of inflexible approach is bound to be defied sooner rather than later. It has the false attraction of simplicity which makes it easy to check performance; it may indeed be generally obeyed for a short time if it is effectively presented by a government as a proper response to a national emergency; but it has the limited staying power that is characteristic of policies which are designed as gestures. The starting point for the kind of approach which appears, on the evidence, to have some prospect of success is the recognition that price increases affect wage settlements in different ways at different times. George Perry in his analysis of American experience up to the mid-1970s reports the following results: 'Empirical estimates covering a long period, such as the past twenty years, indicate that wages are pushed up by only 10 to 20 per cent of past changes in consumer prices. Once inflation has become a prominent issue, however, the impact of living costs on wages may become stronger.'[30] The indications are that the 'pass-through effect' of consumer price increases becomes enormously enlarged once inflation has become a generally established expectation. The argument for tactical short-term intervention by the authorities is then simply that it is worth while trying to avoid that psychological threshold if other measures, fiscal and monetary, with a longer lead time, are brought into operation simultaneously to restore the balance of supply and demand in the economy.

It is curious, indeed, that this subject should have generated quite so much doctrinal fury during the great inflation of the 1970s. To quote Perry again, even though it may be clear to all that a certain established rate of inflation fails to benefit anyone more than another rate established at a lower level, 'individual workers or unions and individual firms and industries cannot, in their own best interest, lead the way to this de-escalation. This is the essence of the case for a government role in slowing the spiral.'[31] That on these straightforward (neo-classical economic) grounds of the rational pursuit of self-interest you may need the government to intervene in the role of honest broker, who identifies the common desire of apparent adversaries and provides the vehicle for its realization by means of agreed collective action, would not of course be a persuasive argument for Hayek and his school. For them the state of inflation is merely an expression of a more profound illness in the economy: to that extent it may even have a certain utility in forcing the attention of those who would prefer to ignore it upon the underlying sickness. It is to be observed that the Hayek view has the great merit, for its propounders, that it cannot be categorically disproved by means of empirical evidence. In this sense it is, again, different from the monetarist argument against the employment of incomes policies; as noted earlier, the evidence of only one case where such policies have been successfully applied without perverse long-term results is sufficient material for its refutation.

To attempt to contradict Hayek's doom-laden analysis by contending that the productive apparatus of the economy is *wholly* responsive to changing demands for goods and services would be foolish. It plainly is not. One can only proceed by asking whether the available, and necessarily partial, data suggest that it has become notably *less* responsive in conditions of sustained high employment. The story of structural adaptation which accompanied the very high rate of economic growth from the early 1960s onwards (recounted in Chapter 1) shows, first of all, that very high levels of employment do not reduce productivity gains. Secondly, there is no indication that during the subsequent period of economic slowdown, when assumptions about the future content and pace of production had to be drastically revised, the high-employment economies, countries like Germany and Japan which had consistently pushed output close to the limits of capacity, were notably more sluggish in adapting to the changed situation than others. Rather the contrary: short-term advantage was not bought at the cost of long-term rigidity. It may seem to be intuitively probable that an economy at or near full employment will be less responsive to changing demand than one which has more slack. But the analysis of economic policy-making is not, fortunately, entirely dependent on the intuitions of theoretical economists.

This is not the place to examine the underlying forces leading to differences in national economic performance. But it is worth saying at this stage that a steady concern on the part of policy-makers with avoiding even a temporary lapse into high unemployment often goes with an active effort to manage longer-term developments in such a way as to help the realization of the objective of full employment. National plans are accordingly laid on the basis of responding rapidly to – and indeed anticipating – possible changes in demand, in relative costs of factors of production, and generally in the international economic environment. National planning agencies have increasingly cultivated a capacity to react sensitively to changes which may require a redirection of economic policy. That means, among other things, limiting the range and fixity of long-term commitments. Intuitions notwithstanding, planners tend to be more responsive than non-planners.[32]

Behind this controversy about incomes policy there lies a more profound difference of view on *how* prices, including the price of labour, are in practice formed. The vision of those who would at any cost avoid intervention by a public body in the business of price determination is essentially the traditional model of an 'auction market'. Here prices are bid up or down by large masses of potential buyers and sellers until they reach the point at which all the supplies available are cleared. This is the most efficient market-clearing mechanism between willing buyers and sellers: each transaction is absolutely discrete and carries no further commitment of any kind from either of the parties towards the other once it has been completed. In contrast, there are what Arthur Okun has called 'customer markets', very familiar in modern practice, in which there is some sort of continuing relationship between buyer and seller. The simplest example is when the sale of some object includes the future performance of certain ancillary services like repair and maintenance. It is noteworthy that very few objects of even moderate value are sold nowadays without a guarantee of some sort to ensure a promised standard of performance for a stated period of time.

'Customer market' relationships are, however, much more widespread and often much less formal than that. The ordinary consumer does not want to treat each purchase that he makes as if it were a fresh event requiring a search and thoroughgoing comparison of a lot of alternative bargains. Such a search implies a costly effort, and although it is done occasionally, most people prefer to set strict limits to this kind of activity. They find it more convenient to establish some relationships of trust with certain sellers, just as the latter will normally take trouble to retain an established customer's goodwill.

All this is very familiar stuff. But it is in fact only by ignoring it, by pretending in effect that there is a zero 'information cost' in buying and no time dimension in the actions of a seller towards his customers, that the classical model of market behaviour and price determination comes to be treated as the norm.

If, as Okun has persuasively shown, 'customer markets' have become very widespread and continue to expand, then the style of commercial behaviour associated with this set of relationships deserves close study. First of all, customers who are looking for 'fair prices' from their regular supplier generally expect him not to take full advantage of temporary shifts in supply and demand to adjust prices, but rather to set these by reference to some fairly constant mark-up on costs. As Okun noted in connection with the empirical findings which showed a high degree of 'mark-up rigidity', this is 'inconsistent with the classical theory of price determination, in which the strength of demand should alter the ratio of prices to costs'.[33] Secondly, the pattern of price inflation when it occurs in such a market is such as to delay movements both up and down. 'Even after excess demand is removed, recent cost increases and wage increases elsewhere will keep pushing up customer prices and career wages.'[34]

In fact, probably the most interesting aspect of this analysis is the effect of the customer type of relationship on labour markets. What Okun calls 'career wages', i.e. those with implicit long-term relationships between employer and employee, are also given to stickiness. Taking on new workers, he points out, and training them, represents a considerable cost to employers. 'Employees become more valuable, but it is impossible to accommodate this fully in a time differential for employees' wages because this would mean lowering the entry wage to the point where it would be uncompetitive with employment in non-career occupations.'

The outcome is that a career employee gets a certain share of the 'joint bonus' from the established relationship; among its consequences is that the employee is encouraged to rely 'on standards of fairness in wage determination whereby the firm's wage structure may be geared to other wages, or to the prices of the firm's products, or to the prices that enter into the worker's cost of living'.[35]

Jobs of the kind described here made up a growing proportion of total employment during the second half of the twentieth century. Their growth may be regarded as a natural accompaniment of the increased demands on the labour force for technical qualifications required for work of increasing complexity, backed by much larger amounts of expensive capital equipment per worker employed. The special benefits offered to 'career workers' may also be seen as developing in parallel with the higher standards of job security and terms of employment obtained by most regular workers in industry and services. The idea of a worker's 'property in his job' came to be widely accepted during the 1960s. The favoured group whose members were regarded by their employers as being difficult and costly to replace were naturally offered still more advantageous conditions. Okun suggests that the commercial success of firms built around customer market pricing and career job strategies during the period of high economic growth fed on itself, through imitation. And one of its consequences which became apparent in the 1970s was that both wages and prices had become less responsive to any given cyclical downturn, or upturn, in business activity.

Thus the benefits that had been gained during the 1960s, when it had been possible to run the economy of the West at a high pressure of demand and to contain, in large measure, the inflationary bias in wages, were achieved by means which later added to the problems of short-term demand management. It became more difficult to curb inflation in a period of slow growth with larger and more frequent business fluctuations. This has implications which reach well beyond the particular circumstances of the 1970s and early 1980s: namely, that once 'customer markets' have become widespread, as they have over the last two decades or so, it is vastly more expensive than in the past, and also more dubious in its effects, to tackle the problem of rising prices by the

traditional instruments of deflation. A low-cost strategy would require that the network of implicit contracts, on which a large part
of the substructure of the economy has come to depend, be
adapted in a systematic way over time to changing economic
circumstances. That is what an incomes policy is chiefly about.[36]

3

The Increasing Complications of Managing an Affluent Economy

After a long period following the Second World War in which the advanced industrial world suffered remarkably little from short-term business cycles — certainly far less than at any time in the recorded history of capitalism — the trouble reasserted itself in the 1970s, and apparently with renewed vigour.[1] The story was subsequently presented as a quarter of a century's holiday from a natural disease, which was only waiting to reappear with its ancient power and rhythm. That at any rate was the version of the traditionalists, whose picture of the world is constructed out of evidence that nothing much under the sun changes as a result of man-made designs, especially in economics. Chapter 2 has given something of the flavour of the debate surrounding the altered circumstances of the 1970s — with one side saying roughly 'We told you so', while the other side insisted that small adjustments to the established instruments of demand management, which had proved their value in happier times, would suffice to restore the old prosperity. Since it will have become abundantly apparent by now where the bias of the author's sympathies lies in this debate, I should make it clear that it does not lead simply to new traditionalism, with its argument that the conditions which established themselves in the second half of the twentieth century remain essentially unchanged, and that the appropriate policy response is the same as in the past, only more of it. This part of my text looks more closely at the changes which can be identified, and asks whether there is evidence that they are getting worse in the sense of rendering the economy more unmanageable.

One such view of progressive unmanageability alleges that although the trouble only became visible to all in the late 1970s, there is evidence going back much further that each business cycle was accompanied by an increase in the rate of inflation as economic activity rose to its peak, and that at each such peak there was progressively higher unemployment. If this were indeed so, it fitted particularly well with the monetarist analysis: pushing activity beyond the level set by the 'natural rate of employment' simply cost more with each successive attempt. As regards unemployment, the data hardly provide convincing evidence for a significant acceleration of this kind.

The OECD report *Interfutures* claims that 'in most OECD countries . . . unemployment rates in the biggest boom years have increased from one cycle to the next'.² Yet an examination of the figures for individual countries during the 1960s shows changes that cannot be regarded as constituting a significant trend. When unemployment rates are around 1 per cent, or below, movements measured in decimals of a percentage point must clearly be treated with a great deal of reserve. A minor alteration in procedures used for collecting the data or the effect of a shift in the composition of the work force, caused for instance by the higher participation rates of women (who may be less determined than men, and are certainly less mobile, in their search for jobs), in conditions where opportunities for employment are plentiful, can produce results of this magnitude. People need only decide, on average, to take two or three days longer in choosing a new job – because they feel that they can afford not to be in quite such a hurry – to cause the statistical movement. With the average worker's income rising steadily and fast, that would be a natural reaction: it is part of having a higher standard of living. As to the 1970s, it is possible that some of the new forces changing the structure of employment (which were discussed earlier in Chapter 1) were already making themselves felt in the boom of 1973. If that were so, it would tell one something about a single unusual event – unusual, among other things, for being a synchronized world boom which moved upward to its peak much faster than any other since the war – not about any long-term development common to the advanced industrial countries.

The evidence on inflation also points to a break, not to a progressive trend. Using indices of consumer prices, the average annual increase from the start of the 1960s in the seven largest OECD countries works out at something under 3 per cent up to and including 1967. This was the outcome of different and opposite movements – a decline in the inflation rate in France and Japan, and a moderate rise towards the end of the period in the USA and Canada. (The average is about the same for the remainder of the OECD, though there are larger differences between individual countries.) [3]

In 1968 the average inflation rate for the major countries moves up to 4 per cent, with the United States setting the higher pace, and raising it still further in the following two years. This was the period when the management of US war finance, in connection with Vietnam, failed; other nations also felt the effect, since the prices of many commodities were fixed in dollars, and it was the dollar price that rose. Later on, with the establishment of the system of flexible exchange rates, it became possible for nations with well-managed domestic finances to escape from this contagious form of inflation by up-valuing their exchange rates; but not at this stage. The result was a rise to a high point of 5½ per cent in 1970; thereafter, as the US brought domestic prices under control, there was a decline in the average rate by a little over 1 per cent.

It is important to fill in the detail because of the subsequent myth that what happened to prices in the 1970s was simply a continuation at an accelerated pace of a trend that had already become well established beforehand. In fact the individual national trends were highly divergent, and both the US and Japan lowered their inflation rates in 1971/2. It was the UK and Germany that were pushing up the pace at this stage; during these two years the German inflation rate was well above the American. The important points to establish in order to straighten out the confused record of these years just before the great inflation are two: first, inflation remained fairly steady at a moderate rate during the years of very rapid growth and full employment up to 1968; secondly, the burst of speed at the end of the 1960s, put on largely under an American impulse, was moderated in advance of the great boom of 1973.[4]

It is in 1973 that the take-off occurs; the rate of inflation doubles in the course of one year – in 1974 prices in the seven major OECD countries rise 13½ per cent, three times the 1972 rate. Even after the slump of 1975 and the check to the rise in real wages, brought on by a variety of national incomes policies, the OECD rate of inflation never goes down to the pre-1973 level.[5]

It is clear that something very special occurred in 1973 – though some of the elements which gave it such exceptional force had been brewing up beforehand. Government policies contributed to the process. The very beginning of the 1970s was a time of *relatively* slow economic advance compared with the years preceding it. Considered in retrospect, it has the appearance of little more than a minor fluctuation around a very high growth rate. But given the exigent standards which the preceding prosperity had established, the result was seen by some governments as reflecting a failure of economic policy to respond sensitively enough to a changing situation. There was talk of the symptoms of a 'mini-recession', a phrase which well expresses the spirit which prepared the ground for the over-stimulation that was a characteristic feature of the subsequent boom. Production in the West rose, under the impulse of expansionist policies, at a breakneck pace; and this was combined with an exceptional movement of funds into international capital markets – prompted by the vast American balance of payments deficit and the general weakness of the US dollar in foreign exchange markets – which was rapidly converted into a torrent of liquid resources feeding the domestic money supply in many countries. Governments had not quite realized how open their economies had become and how sensitive to movements of money generated beyond their own borders. Some nations, like Germany, were more sensitive to these developments than others, but there were few which responded in time. The novelty of the situation faced by governments was another factor contributing to the general failure of short-term demand management at this stage.

The mechanics of the recession which followed had some novel features. Policy-makers could hardly be blamed for not anticipating that the consequences of the oil price shock would be, first of all, a further huge increase in wage incomes at the expense of profits, and secondly that a large part of the additional personal income would be saved and not spent. Demand accordingly collapsed on two fronts simultaneously – investment dropped with the fall in profits, while there was no additional demand for consumer goods and services from the recipients of higher wage incomes.

The remarkable performance of personal savings, which prompted pressures for fiscal action to sustain demand just at the time when governments were in a mood of some contrition about their earlier policy of economic over-stimulation, is worth considering a little more closely, in terms of the psychological factor in business cycle policy-making. Having overreacted previously, policy-makers now underreacted to the collapse in demand. They had, not unreasonably, assumed that wage-earners, with considerably enlarged money incomes at a time of rapidly rising prices, would be strongly inclined to convert the extra cash into purchases of real goods. Instead, they did the opposite – they delayed purchases of items that could be readily postponed and were inclined to pare down even their ordinary household expenditure in real terms, in order, apparently, to give themselves a larger margin of ready cash or nearly liquid resources. In some respects this was the first significant test of the behaviour of the *new* working class which had ceased altogether, during the previous quarter of a century, to be, and to feel, proletarian, in the literal sense of being without significant assets other than current earnings when its finances were threatened. Substantial minimum standards of living had been secured in the interval through unemployment benefits and other welfare payments; so that risks of hardship were reduced. The general expectation was that wage-earners would go on spending their incomes in their accustomed ways even it if meant reducing the amount which they normally saved. They were, after all, pretty well insured against serious adversity.

The opposite reaction, in so far as its deeper motivation could be traced and analysed,[6] reflected a rational response to increased anxiety of a new type; to maintain the capacity to meet unforeseen contingencies personal command over liquid resources had to be maintained in real terms. That was the first priority. It meant that in money terms more had to be saved, in the short period, in order to restore the purchasing power of existing savings. It is of course not clear that affluent wage-earners will necessarily always behave in the same fashion in similar circumstances. There are several factors which may influence the outcome in different ways, including the degree of uncertainty about the likely opportunities for well-paid employment in the future, and the amount of unemployment pay available to meet anticipated personal and family needs.

The United States, in fact, offered an interesting variation in savings behaviour from the other OECD countries from the mid-1970s onwards. Whereas personal savings continued in most countries at a high level – though somewhat below the peak rate reached at the depth of the slump – the Americans saved less and less out of their current income. They were, it is true, in a phase of extremely rapid expansion, especially of employment, in contrast to the sluggish conditions elsewhere. Indeed, the later stages of the American boom in 1978/9 were largely sustained by this high rate of dis-saving. But even when the economy had visibly turned down in early 1980, the process continued to such an extent that the Federal Reserve Board felt it necessary to take special action to cut supplies of particular forms of credit which were used by banks and other credit institutions to give support to consumers in their spendthrift mood.[7] It was an extreme form of discrimination, undertaken reluctantly and justified only by the need to compel American consumers to behave like people should when they are faced with a substantial loss of income in a slump (not mitigated this time in any way by tax reductions). The trouble was that the American, unlike his European counterpart, was more impressed by the actual and prospective fall in the value of money than by the cut in his personal income. He had to be positively bludgeoned into thrift, before he responded as he was supposed to do.

Two Recessions of the 1970s Compared

The story of the contrasting behaviour of American and other consumers aptly illustrates the problems of managing the business cycles of the 1970s. The uncertainties were no less in the second economic downturn which, against the wishes and expectations of the US Government, which had intended to run a purely private short recession on its own, became general in 1979/80. It is of some interest to compare the two business cycles and the policies which were applied to them. Some of the similarities and differences were listed by the OECD in mid-1980; the table is appended here, pp. 94–7. It summarizes usefully the reasons which were advanced at the time for increased optimism about economic policy during the second cycle. The first important difference which emerges is that the high point of economic activity reached in 1979 represented a much lower pressure of demand on available resources. The 1973 boom, as was observed earlier, was an extreme version of a great surge of spending, which led to production bottlenecks, the piling up of excessive stocks, and steeply rising prices in commodity markets, as buyers scrambled for supplies. Business behaviour at the end of the 1970s was extremely sedate by comparison. It should therefore have been an easier business cycle for the authorities to cope with.

Secondly, the high rate of inflation which continued and was, initially, reinforced during the economic slowdown was a novelty in the first business cycle. It had become an established phenomenon by the end of the 1970s, and it seemed a safe bet that it would persist for some time longer. This also had the effect of making the policy-makers, somewhat paradoxically, more confident. While the monetary authorities were, as the OECD observed, acting in a more systematic fashion to check domestic inflation, it was also assumed generally – as it was not during the early 1970s – that the upward trend of prices would be maintained. That in turn was taken to imply that both businesses and ordinary consumers would go on spending cash in order to acquire real assets, even though the economic downturn squeezed current incomes all round[8] And this led to the conclusion that governments would need to intervene less than in the first business cycle if they wished to maintain the aggregate level of demand. Hence the interesting prediction made in the document reproduced in the Appendix that the 'tight' monetary and fiscal policy would not be relaxed with the decline in economic activity, as it had been in 1975. This is a striking example of the way in which essentially psychological assumptions of an uncertain kind intrude into apparently rigorous economic argument. The real point at issue was how nervous people were likely to become, as unemployment rose throughout the Western world to levels substantially higher than anything experienced before in the second half of the twentieth century. Would businessmen and consumers follow the American or the European (and Japanese) pattern of behaviour? It seemed on the face of it just a little too comfortable for governments to assume that the victims of the slump could be relied upon to spend their way out of it because they were assured that it would be an inflationary slump.

There were other reasons for the mood of self-restraint in the exercise of counter-cyclical policies by governments, correctly noted by the OECD, at the start of the 1980s. After the first oil shock in 1973 Western governments were much more uncertain about what had hit them and about how long the deeper trouble of coping with a cartel of producers of the industrial countries' key commodity would last. They also evinced a stronger impulse to act together in seeking ways of limiting the damage to their collective economic performance that would be caused by allowing the full force of the shock to strike home all at once. The impact was to be cushioned; the effects on prices and incomes of the sudden rise in the cost of energy were to be spread out over time. There was a general fear of an excessive deflationary response, which would surely follow if each nation sought to achieve as rapidly as possible the transfer of real resources to the oil producers, required to restore the balance in its external payments.[9]

In the event the Western nations failed to manage the change without a fall in their combined output in 1975. They also failed entirely to co-ordinate their balance of payments policies. Britain and a few other countries made a deliberate effort to sustain domestic economic activity and to counter the effect of an externally generated drop in demand; their consequent balance of payments deficits were enlarged as a result of the opposite policies followed by Germany in particular, which gave priority to the objective of restoring its external payments to equilibrium with the utmost speed. Helped by the fact that its neighbours, particularly those in north-west Europe, were pursuing different objectives, Germany's well-established advantages in international trade competition were reinforced, and took the country rapidly into massive balance of payments surplus.[10]

At the same time, it is arguable that the Western nations were altogether *too* successful in protecting their consumers from the direct effects of the rise in the price of energy. They were able to do this partly because so large a part of the domestic cost of oil products in particular consisted of taxes. The outcome of this, and of other factors which are discussed below, was that the *real* price of energy for internal use in the major industrial countries rose by less than 15 per cent between 1973 and 1978.[11] This extremely modest response to a 350 per cent rise in the cost of oil imports in 1973/4 reflected in part the large concomitant increases in the cost of other items in consumer budgets. (The 'real cost' is measured by dividing the energy component in the consumer price index by the total index of consumer prices.) In this sense the general inflation of locally produced goods and services in Western countries helped to mask the profound change in the cost of this key element in the Western standard of living. It also served to provide some relief to the oil-importing economies from the massive additional charge placed upon them by the oil exporters. This happened because after the initial massive price increase imposed by OPEC, the dollar price of internationally traded oil remained fairly stable, and even declined a little, as demand weakened with the economic slowdown in the Western world, while export prices of Western manufactured goods rose rapidly. By 1978 they were roughly double what they had been just before the first oil shock.[12] Thus nearly one-half of the additional burden on the Western balance of payments, caused by the movement of the terms of trade in favour of the oil producers, had been eliminated at the same time as the volume of Western manufactured goods exported to the oil-producing countries vastly increased. The opportunity cost of producing these exports was relatively low in the sluggish business conditions ruling at the time, since a substantial part of the resources used, labour and capital, would otherwise probably have remained unemployed.

This relatively painless way of dealing with oil shock, by means of inflation and of a number of *ad hoc* measures which limited the effect of rising fuel costs on household budgets, was not the outcome of a conscious choice by Western governments. In the end, it is fair to say, the policy-makers were less impressed by their success in avoiding serious trouble than by the inconveniences of the heritage of inflation and distorted prices which it left behind. Nevertheless, an assessment of these years of improvisation and fumbling in the middle and late 1970s must register the fact that a profound disturbance to the industrial system of the West was in the event absorbed with remarkably little social strain. Those who had witnessed the radical upsurge at the end of the 1960s, associated with the students' movement and industrial workers' demands, and had noted the apparent readiness of the protesters to reject the existing social order, were surprised. The welfare state, when it was put to the test, did, after all, demonstrate a capacity for making the transition to slower economic growth and higher unemployment politically manageable.

One of the questions raised by the change in the policy stance which characterized the reaction to the second oil shock at the end of the 1970s is whether governments had come to take this remarkably cool climate of social relations in a period of strain rather too easily for granted. The political issue was put well by Samuel Brittan, an influential British advocate of a rigorous monetarist approach to the management of inflation and harsh critic of policies of compromise. In a discussion of the 'political economy of inflation' [13] he commented with disarming frankness on the way in which the struggle between different interest groups over the distribution of income and wealth was, after all, rendered less brutal through the 'temporary solvent' of inflation. He concluded with the observation that the period in which the cosy politics of disguising changes in relative shares of income and wealth by permitting prices to rise might 'come to appear the hallmark if not of a golden, at least of a silver age'. It is legitimate to add that the nostalgia of those who do not share Brittan's monetarist view of how prices are formed in contemporary society, but believe that 'customer markets' must, if prices are to be better controlled, be tackled on their own terms, would be that much stronger.

But these were not the considerations which influenced the approach of policy-makers to the second business cycle of the 1970s. They felt that they had, with a few exceptions of which Germany was held up as the shining example, mismanaged the first cycle by being altogether too permissive. Now they went to the opposite extreme: there was to be the minimum of delay, or concession to social welfare, in enforcing those changes in the Western economies implied by the need to transfer to the oil producers the additional real resources (required to pay for the doubling of the oil price in 1979).[14] Gradualism, the guiding principle of the early 1970s, was out. The subtraction of the resources from the Western economies needed for the transfer had to be quick and complete, with little regard for the effect on economic activity in the West. And the fact that the oil-exporting nations were most unlikely to absorb at short notice the large additional volume of resources, which the West was intent on denying itself, was also disregarded. Here again the prospect was different, and less favourable, than it had been after the first oil shock. This was partly because many of the oil producers had already gone on a large-scale spending spree and now had neither the inclination, nor in some instances the physical capacity, to absorb vast additional amounts of Western manufactured goods at short notice.

The International Dimension

All told, the international economic environment which provided the context for the second business cycle was distinctly less favourable than it had been for the first. This despite the fact that the Western countries managed at the end of the 1970s, largely through the accidents of timing of the various turns in national economic policy, to avoid the closely synchronized international upturn and downturn of business which had so aggravated the troubles of the early 1970s. The main point was that the trading opportunities of the rest of the world had diminished, in relative terms, during the interval. It was not only the rich oil-exporting countries of the Third World whose markets had become less responsive; the other developing countries, for quite different reasons, had less purchasing power. They had come to rely very heavily during the second half of the 1970s on international borrowing to sustain their imports. Indeed, the non-oil developing countries managed, despite the difficulties for their trade created by the economic slowdown in the West, to increase their share of world imports. It was not generally recognized at the time that these countries had played a significant role in maintaining the buoyancy of Western trade during a difficult period. Trade among the OECD group of advanced industrial countries, which had been the dynamic factor in the major expansion of international trade in the first quarter of a century following the Second World War, declined sharply as a share of the world total during the five years following the collapse of the 1973 boom.[15] The Soviet bloc had also provided a good market for the exports of the industrial countries in the 1970s, again substantially financed by international loans. Though not as important as the non-oil developing countries, which absorbed nearly half of the total of international lending (in 1979 they borrowed 64 billion dollars, nearly four times the 1973 total), the Soviet bloc countries taken together had been significant borrowers. Individual countries like Poland drew very heavily indeed on the international capital market, to an extent which contributed to the economic crisis which overtook that country in 1980.[16]

Both in the Soviet bloc and in the Third World an increasing part of the borrowings from the West was being used to service earlier loans. It was already plain before the end of the 1970s that it would not be possible to maintain anything like the previous growth of loan-financed imports from the Western industrial countries during the 1980s. The international banking system, in the view of some of the key persons and institutions involved, was already dangerously stretched: the danger lay in the possibility that one or two defaults could lead to a cumulative collapse, as lenders scrambled to withdraw their deposits. It was true that, in part responding to this fear, the bankers and the monetary authorities of Western countries went to very great lengths to ensure that no significant debtor country was put under such pressure that it was seriously tempted to refuse to meet its debt-servicing obligations. There was a kind of conspiracy among the creditors to maintain the morale, and the hopes, of bankrupt or near-bankrupt nations. But in the meanwhile the constraint of prudence in making new loans to countries, whose credit-worthiness was visibly dwindling with the rise in their debt-servicing commitments, was reinforced. Moreover, the world's bankers experienced this mood of nervousness at a time when a lot of new business from other, more attractive, borrowers in the developed countries, victims of the deficits caused by the sudden rise in their oil import bills, was coming forward. The upshot was that exporters in the OECD countries seemed likely to find fewer buyers outside, not only during the imminent downturn of the business cycle but also for a longer time to come. And inside the OECD, the dynamic rise of exports, which had depended on the combination of a sustained US balance of payments deficit and the systematic removal of import barriers, showed no prospect of being resumed. The tariffs on industrial goods were already so low that shaving them a bit further would not make much difference, and the United States had ceased to be in a position where it could permit the rest of the industrial world to be in chronic surplus with it. In fact, neither side could afford to let that continue.

Another important change of longer-term significance was the shift in the international balance of economic power at the end of the 1970s. While the business cycle in the Western countries had indeed been successfully de-synchronized, the circumstances in which this had been accomplished were not propitious for the future of concerted international policy-making. As has already been noted, there was not, in spite of the rhetoric of the OECD, any strong interest among the leading industrial nations in the practice of systematic 'concertation' by the time the decade drew to a close. Economic virtue 1979/80 style consisted in each nation giving its full attention to looking after its own backyard on the lines indicated by a common, and fairly severe, monetary drillbook.[17] The particular numbers which triggered off the appropriate drillbook responses differed from one country to another, but the underlying idea was the same. In essence, the sergeant-majors of the system, the central bankers, who really knew about the detailed management of regimental manoeuvres, were to take over more responsibility from the political generals who, it was felt, had failed to concentrate effectively on the task.

The United States became an enthusiastic practitioner of the new

style. The members of President Carter's original team of policy-
makers, including their intellectual leader Charles Schultze, the
notable Keynesian economist who was chairman of the President's
Council of Economic Advisers, still made their voices heard, but
in practical terms they were increasingly overshadowed by the
dominant figure of the chairman of the Federal Reserve Board, Mr
Volcker. It had become clear at the end of the 1970s that the
United States would have to deflate its extremely buoyant economy more than had been originally intended, in order to bring its
balance of payments deficit under control. The long boom proved
remarkably resilient in its later stages, partly because, as noted,
American consumers saved less and spent more. Under the leadership of Volcker, brought in to head the Federal Reserve Board
during the dollar crisis of 1970, the United States proceeded actively to induce an economic recession in order to restore confidence in the dollar. It was impelled to do so in part because the
decline in the exchange parity of the dollar (which was in fact
caused chiefly by the adverse turn in the nation's capital account,
as investors diversified their dollar portfolios into other currencies)
aggravated the already substantial rise in American prices. Higher
world grain prices, which were caused by poor harvests elsewhere
but whose effect the Americans, as the world's largest exporters of
cereals, could not escape, coincided with the rise in oil prices (as
had happened in 1973/4). These commodity price movements, over
neither of which the United States had any control, came on top
of a sharp, but not extraordinary, increase in domestic inflation
which accompanied the tail-end of a sustained and vigorous
boom.[18]

It was not difficult to understand the mood of overkill which
guided the American response. The United States had earlier tried
to conduct a policy of all-out expansion, regardless of the size and
cost of its bill for imported energy and other products. After the
painful experience of being stopped in its tracks, the US government was not ready to try to lead the world out of recession once
again. There was neither the capacity nor the desire to do so. This
marked a more important change in the substructure of international economic relations than was perhaps generally realized at
the time. America, having failed, in spite of its exceptional eco-

nomic and political resources, to get the Western world back on to the path of self-sustaining growth, discovered that it had instead become weakened and economically isolated in the process. Running its own business cycle into a phase of expansion out of step with its trading partners and allies in the Western world had proved to be an operation beyond its capacity. The shock of discovery was painful. The United States, for all its size and magnificence, was, it had been shown, just another industrial nation, more important and powerful but not different in other ways from the rest. The American reaction suggested that, at the very least, this was likely to lead to a lower propensity on the part of the United States to take economic risks in the style to which the Western world had in the previous forty years become accustomed. It was not clear that the West could readily conduct its affairs on that basis. At a time when long-established stances, based on a set of economic assumptions deriving from the dominant position of an international currency managed by the world's most powerful nation, had come to look shaky, the faculty of leadership could not be readily dispensed with. Charles Kindleberger has shown how important this particular feature of international relations has been at political turning points in the world economy, like the onset of the great depression in 1929.[19] If the 1980s proved to be a more unstable period in international economic relations, as well as one with more frequent economic fluctuations and a slower pace of growth, then the requirements of international consensus among the leading countries were likely to be more demanding than in the past. Leadership in organizing such a consensus would in that case be at a high premium.

Long-term Changes

The examination of the international dimension thus points to changes between the two business cycles of the 1970s which promise to be of a more durable character. There are other changes observable inside the domestic social and economic systems of Western countries which point in a similar direction. It is not suggested that these developments are new reoulting in some sense from the special circumstances of the years of difficulty and economic slowdown which followed the quarter of a century of progress in highly favourable circumstances after the Second World War. A number of the problems existed in the earlier period; they manifested themselves in a much more acute form, however, once the economic environment became less favourable. (We have already noted how this occurred in regard to industry as a declining source of employment.) But the reinforced perception of economic change brings its own special economic consequences. They affect the behaviour of both labour and capital, but more powerfully the latter.

It is obvious that the decision to invest or not to invest in productive enterprise is more profoundly affected by expectations that are closely calculated than the decision whether to work or not at a given wage. The second type of decision is very largely determined by established conventions – though, with the change in the composition of the labour force and the *style* of working, decisions in this sphere, too, are more closely influenced by perceptions of the longer-term prospect than they were in the past. This is another way of saying that the day-to-day pressures to take a job which yields a living wage are less insistent. That is one of the consequences of the advance of the welfare state, in which not merely the right to work but the right to choose a job according with an individual's taste and views of his own ability has been in process of being established. It has gone much farther in some countries than in others; but the extension of the notion of the right to work in this manner is a common phenomenon of Western industrial societies.

There are other developments of a social character which have made employment for a growing proportion of the working population more of an optional choice than in the past. And the underlying changes in work habits have occurred in an extremely short time. A few illustrative figures will suffice to make the point. In the United States, which is much the biggest employer of labour among the nations of the Western industrial world, the proportion of households made up of couples in which both members were wage- or salary-earners increased from 42 per cent in 1958 to 59 per cent in 1975.[20] The growth of part-time employment is a reflection of the same process of the massive entry of women into the labour force. It is estimated that in a number of the advanced industrial countries above one-sixth of all the job opportunities in the late 1970s were part-time, and that the number of such jobs had increased by some 40-50 per cent in the previous ten years.[21]

Such a shift in the pattern of employment gives rise to a variety of effects. I shall mention two only. One is that the spending of the second working member of the household tends to have a discretionary character: it varies more. It will also be more sensitive to fluctuations in marginal employment opportunities with the ups and downs of the business cycle. In addition to the influence on the pattern of demand, two-job families exercise an influence on the supply side of the economy, because in such a family the attachment of each person to his or her job makes the other that much more immobile. Immobility, which tends in any case to be enhanced by the incidental features of affluence, is further reinforced when both the man and the woman at the head of a household are employed in jobs with career opportunities.

The enlargement of choice and of personal opportunities probably has the general effect of making the economies of the rich Western nations less responsive to change. People with a high level of unemployment pay tend to spend more time in the search for a new job which is to their liking, when they lose or leave the old one, than in the past. It is a commonplace that the amount of frictional unemployment rises with affluence – and so it should: the great advance in the standard of living of the age of acceleration would be largely devoid of significance if people were not able to be more deliberate in making some of the most important choices in their lives. The middle classes have always acted in this way.

In the same spirit members of middle-class professions have traditionally fixed minimum fees or salaries, frequently with the backing of a professional association. Now that this has become a regular feature of working-class employment, it adds another element of inflexibility to the productive performance of the economy. Jobs which cannot yield an attractive profit to an employer at the minimum wage are not performed – or are performed in an irregular fashion by workers operating in the 'black economy'. It is arguable that the latter simply provide the additional element of flexibility which society through its wrong-headed decisions has denied itself.[22] But this is almost certainly not the most efficient way of using productive resources. It is a highly perverse consequence of the great advance in public welfare standards and the general acceptance of the need to protect those who are likely to be weak bargainers in an employment situation, that these praiseworthy turns of events deny some people who are willing to work the opportunity to produce. Moreover, the minimum wage need not be explicitly legislated; the same result is achieved by a guaranteed payment for not working, in the form of unemployment compensation, at a level well above subsistence. The effect is then considerably reinforced through the power of trade unions which frequently fix differentials between the minimum wage and that paid to their members; they also make it their business to establish effective control over the supply of labour flowing into a number of occupations favoured by differentials of this kind.

Broadly, there were two different and opposite approaches to the problem, when it became prominent with the slackening of the demand for labour in the 1970s. One was to embark on a systematic reversal of the forces which interfered with the operation of a free market in labour. Unhappily, this also required, if it were to be properly done, the dismantling of a large part of the structure of the welfare state which had been built up in the previous twenty-five years. Merely weakening the monopolistic power of trade unions to bid up wages beyond the value of the marginal product of labour would not suffice. The operation of public power aimed at protecting living standards at existing minimum levels would have to be directly reduced.[23] On the other side, the defenders of social reform, who were aware of the perverse effect of the advance in welfare on the market for labour, proposed that the problem be met by *more* government intervention – working with market forces, rather than against them. The advance of social welfare required that certain transactions be withdrawn from the sphere of the market – just as developed democracies circumscribe the freedom of individuals to buy and sell votes for money in an election. However, while the *sphere* of markets is confined in various ways with the advance of civilization, market *processes* may well be reinforced in the interests of general welfare. An obvious example is the more active use of anti-trust law, a notable development of economic policy in Western Europe during the 1960s and 1970s, to protect consumers from the whims, or worse, of over-powerful suppliers by establishing the conditions of a competitive market place.

The sense that a number of different forces, some of them deriving from deeper origins than the incidents of social welfare engineering, were combining to reduce the capacity of Western economies to create wealth was widespread in the 1970s. Initially at any rate there was also the feeling that the intelligent application of more capital investment with more scientific power behind it should be able to make good the loss of some of the simple industrial prowess of the 1950s and 1960s. There were obvious opportunities, deriving from advances in industrial technology, for doing precisely this. Indeed, there was something slightly paradoxical about the juxtaposition of the fears concerning the ability of advanced machines to produce so much more with the aid of less human effort, side by side with the anxiety about the general loss of economic potency. The image it suggests is that of a mighty eunuch.

Whence the feeling of impotence? There were several different strands in this common sentiment of Western society. One in particular which seems significant is worth following through. It begins with the increasing share of total output going into labour incomes. As we have seen, there were special circumstances right at the end of the 1960s which led to an effective series of demands by wage-earners for a bigger share of output. But the story goes back further than this. During the earlier period of post-war expansion productivity in a number of countries rose faster than the increase in wages. The capitalists had never had it so good. And the great investment boom and the acceleration of productive activity in the 1960s followed.

Productivity of Capital

However, the earlier basis for the share-out between capital and labour was not maintained. Even in the early years of the 1960s there is evidence in some countries, notably Germany, of a decline

in the productivity of capital, in the sense that each additional unit
of productive capital invested yielded a smaller increase in real
national product. The German figures show an average annual rate
of decline of 1.3 per cent from 1963 until the end of the decade.[24]
In Britain there was a similar, and even steeper, downward trend.
Meanwhile the productivity of labour continued its rapid rise. It
simply required more capital input per man-hour worked to produce the result.

There are a variety of possible reasons for this trend. One is
that the productive capital came to be less intensively employed.
There is some evidence that this was one of the incidental consequences of the very marked reduction in working hours in Germany – a movement which was general among all industrial countries, but in which the Germans led the way. Another contributory
factor could well have been the general shift in the balance of
economic activity towards the service trades, with a smaller share
of total output coming from manufacturing industry. The underlying trend, which was present earlier, became especially marked
during the 1970s. Now capital invested in manufacturing with
characteristically large, and often increasing, economies of scale
tends in general to be more productive than when it is invested in
services. So does labour. This is not to ignore some of the impres-
sive productivity gains achieved in services such as sea and air
transport. But it is true, and significant, as a broad generalization.

There is a further structural change in the content of production
which has also had some effect in reducing the productivity of
capital in advanced European industrial countries like Germany.
It is another aspect of the 'product cycle'. As the Bundesbank observes in its analysis of the trend with particular reference to the
1970s, investment in innovative methods with a high return was
cheaper when businesses were taking over and applying a well-
established technology, usually developed in North America.[25] It
becomes notably more expensive, especially in terms of additional
research and development costs, when nations have to turn to a
do-it-yourself style of innovation.[26] There has in fact been a significant rise in the proportion of German national output devoted
to research and development during the 1970s.[27]

Added to the various forces making business investment in the expansion of output a less attractive option than it was earlier was the decline, during much of the 1970s, of the share of profits at the expense of wages incomes. This was not true everywhere: the United States was a notable exception. But it was a trend which was sufficiently widespread to affect both the pace and the content of investment. To the extent that labour had become more expensive through its ability to keep wages rising in line with total productivity gains, while the relative return to capital declined, a business strategy which successfully replaced labour by applying more capital investment to the same volume of output was that much more attractive. Of course, saving labour by means of better technology and organization has been the basis for the advance of industrial societies from their beginning. The situation was, however, different when the increase in productive power was normally associated with rising total production, facilitating economies of scale. The notable feature of the 1970s was that, at least in Europe and Japan, investment in secondary industry was associated with a decline in the number of workers engaged in industrial production. More strikingly, this trend was observed before the economic slowdown, precisely during the very rapid advance in the years leading up to the 1973 peak of the boom. Then, in the changed business climate, with the prospect for the growth of markets looking much more uncertain, there were additional causes for hesitation and delay. In this way the effects of sluggish economic growth gave rise to familiar cumulative effects. There was certainly nothing novel about this situation. It was characteristic of the turning points leading to a downswing in the long business cycles of the past – such as the early 1870s and the late 1920s. The question is whether we are indeed heading for a similar cyclical pattern in the 1980s.

For our present purposes, in relation to the problems of short-term economic management, there are two aspects of the change in circumstances which are worthy of particular attention. The first is that if, as appears probable from a study of the two short business cycles of the 1970s, the economy is less given to generating its own spontaneous process of revival, then more active intervention will be required from governments to lift the level of demand. Secondly, such intervention may well have to be sustained for a longer time. Stubborn persistence in pump-priming may be necessary to convince business investors that it is indeed worth taking what will look like an enhanced risk. In Keynesian language, what I am saying is that when, as in the late 1970s, the marginal efficiency of capital declines, the problem is to change *long-term* profit expectations. Governments have to appear as credible interventionists, who can be relied upon to offset probable deficiencies of private demand and mitigate the risks of sudden and uncontrollable increases in the costs of certain inputs – energy being the prime example, but not necessarily a unique case – which may put a severe and long-lasting squeeze on profits.

All this points to a more interventionist, risk-taking, entrepreneurial state – an image which does not sit easily with the prevailing climate of politics at the start of the 1980s. To make matters worse, the forms of intervention required for short-term demand management tend to be more tactical and discriminatory, in order to meet the new problems created by changes in the world economy. That follows essentially from the fact that it is more difficult to exercise control by means of traditional economic devices on societies which have become both more affluent and more open.

Measures which operate with reasonable success in a closed economy, or at any rate one which is little influenced in the short term by shifts in international transactions, may be countered by their secondary effects on a vast and volatile international capital market. Thus a country with a strong currency which puts a squeeze on the money supply and raises interest rates, as part of an effort to damp down a rise in domestic demand which is judged to be excessive, finds that the effect is to attract a large inflow of funds from abroad which adds to the liquid resources of the banking system. This is what happened on a number of occasions in the 1960s and 1970s, most especially in Germany. The response of the authorities there was to impose further regulations on the banking system. To make the domestic monetary policy work, funds which originated abroad had to be carefully segregated; then the banks holding them were subjected to different and more severe reserve requirements on these funds; and when, as happened on occasion, this deterrent did not work, the authorities issued orders prohibiting the payment of interest on foreign accounts. They even went so far as to penalize the foreigner who persisted in his urge to hold D-Marks by charging him a fee – imposing in effect a negative rate of interest.

It is a notable fact that the freeing of international markets in currency tended to induce governments to engage in more, rather than less, interventionist activity. This was one of the less expected results of the general move to flexible rates of exchange in the early 1970s. It was hailed at the time as a major achievement of the more liberal international order, which was supposed to liberate citizens from the nuisance of being subjected to government interfering with transactions because of their effect on the nation's external balance of payments. With floating exchange rates, it was argued, the ebb and flow of foreign currency entering into the balance of payments would be dealt with by appropriate alterations in the value of individual currencies, determined by market forces. In the event governments were not prepared, rather predictably, to allow this key variable, which they regarded as an important instrument of national policy, to slip from their control. They intervened more actively than ever in foreign exchange markets, through their central banks, to ensure that it did not. Other, more direct, means were also used, as indicated above, to achieve the same purpose.

Governable Economies

It is not that economies have become ungovernable – so unresponsive to short-term demand management that it is not worth the effort of trying. In the second half of the 1970s this sentiment became widespread. Indeed, it achieved a certain sophisticated support from an influential school of economists, who argued that Keynesian methods of intervention were doomed to be frustrated because 'rational expectations', entertained by economic actors whom they are intended to influence, will systematically negate their effect.[28] In fact, the later years of the 1970s were a time when President Carter's Administration set out, in a period of deep slump, to create a high employment boom, and did so; and when Germany, under international pressure, set out to boost a flagging economy to a higher level of investment activity, and did so. Moreover, the international effects of the German action from 1978 onwards, combined with the additional stimulus applied to Japanese domestic spending at the same time (also prompted by the agreement of governments to embark on the policy of 'concerted action' at the summit meeting in Bonn in mid-1978), were fully in line with what the policy-makers had intended. The plan was that the countries with the strongest balance of payments would move first, and, as the consequences of their actions strengthened the export performance of other OECD countries in close trade relations with them, the latter would be enabled to embark on bolder policies of domestic expansion. It was a demanding operation of timing to launch this two-stage rocket in the international economy, probably a unique operation of its kind. The benign results of the second stage were already beginning to make themselves felt in a growing number of countries when, as we have seen, the oil shock of 1979 disrupted the process.

Thus the ultimate efficacy of the method, when circumstances were favourable, was not put in doubt. The difficulties about its application, however, seemed to multiply. For one thing, the whole process of applying a push or a pull-back to a modern economy proved to be a much rougher and more approximate operation than the original practitioners of demand management had assumed. There was a built-in tendency to undershoot or overshoot targets. Governments, whose desire for a moderate form of intervention was well expressed by their favourite imagery of a motor car – 'a touch of the brake' or 'a little pressure on the accelerator' – found instead that they were under the necessity of employing a battering-ram or some large piece of earth-moving equipment. In these circumstances they become reluctant, and they hesitate.

And that points to another political problem: the instruments are not only big and clumsy but also slow-moving. Their effective performance requires persistence by the policy-makers. Again, there is a delicate problem of timing because the 'electoral cycle' may not leave a government with enough time to apply its chosen measures in a deliberate and sustained manner. There is a tendency for action to be delayed too long and then to become hectic in the face of an imminent election.[29] Finally there is the consideration, running in some degree counter to the demand for stubborn persistence in policy making, that its objects nowadays are a moving target. Established relationships between the component parts of the economic system are changing, as people, their personal habits and the environment in which they live, undergo profound alterations. Worse still for the forecaster, the changes may be profound and yet not last very long. We have seen examples of such uncertainties in the behaviour of personal savings during the 1970s. The influence of the changing international environment is an equally powerful destroyer of stable expectations. Pity the poor econometrician who feeds a government with subtle equations based on the carefully garnered statistics of a past series of economic fluctuations. But pity the government even more!

It is no wonder perhaps that the idea of short-term economic management as a means of riding over business cycles had come to be treated with increasing suspicion by the end of the 1970s. Here, in the tension between the more demanding requirements for effective intervention and the increased uncertainties about the behaviour of the objects being interfered with, lies one of the sources of the sentiment of impotence which I remarked upon earlier. The logic of an extension of the scope and activity of public power contradicted governmental self-distrust. It was not that politicians had suddenly changed their nature and developed a lack of confidence in their own abilities. One hardly needs to remind oneself that there was once a political party in New York which proudly called itself 'Know Nothings'. The hesitations of the third quarter of the twentieth century derived rather from the permanent apparatus of government, from the high bureaucrats in the extensive network of public agencies. These people made up a force that politicians had to reckon with, and they also exercised an important, though diffuse, influence on the views of politicians in office about the limits of public power.

Was the lesson to be learned that these limits were so severe that the proper policy for governments was one of systematic abstention? Much of the sentiment behind the modish political monetarism of the period derived from a bias in this direction. Governments could not of course opt out of ultimate responsibility, but it was believed by adherents of this school of thought that there was a better-than-even chance that some other force, usually referred to under the omnibus title of 'the market', would manage almost any problem better than a government. Monetarist economics, as preached so effectively by Milton Friedman, offered the great attraction of requiring of governments only a very small number of decisions – in fact one major one, about maintaining a fixed and modest increase in the money supply from year to year, from which most of the rest followed. However, even in this case it required more than a policy of abstaining from making decisions to arrive at the blessed state in which decisions would no longer be necessary. In the meantime, monetary policy judgements would have to be made about the appropriate size of the input to the money supply in the light of (monetary) information about the short-term movement of the economy. Since such information is at best six months to a year old and, furthermore, changes in monetary aggregates are not quick-acting, suffering from delays (as their proponents have shown) of up to two years, the operation would be subject to the same weakness as more traditional forms of demand management.

Even after the state of monetary equilibrium, in Friedman's sense, had been reached, there is something deeply unrealistic in the notion that governments would in practice refrain, during some emergency caused by an external shock or an internal disaster, whether natural or man-made, from using the potent instrument of varying the supply of money, because of the danger that inflation might emerge again in the long run. Man-made business cycle disasters, involving unemployment at around 10 per cent, would be likely to pose just such an irresistible challenge to the policy of monetary quietism. Indeed, a rational calculation of the risks, at a reasonable rate of discount applied to the troubles of the future, made by a committed monetarist might well lead to the same result. As an OECD survey of *The Role of Monetary Policy in Demand Management* in the post-war period wisely concluded, 'the potential contribution of monetary policy over a 6–12 months horizon has been so considerable as to make it unlikely that the disadvantages of long-term instability could outweigh it.'[30]

There is in fact no short cut through the problems discussed in this chapter. The reaction against the earlier pretension of omnicompetence of certain governments is understandable, and the particular rejection of 'fine tuning' of the economy by Keynesian methods of demand management is fully sustained by the post-war evidence of failure. But it has been followed by a movement, which seems likely to prove just as untenable, to the other extreme.

There are other aspects of the matter besides demand management, in particular the conduct of medium- and long-term economic policy. The issue of defining the scope and limits of government in the changed circumstances which emerged in the fourth decade after the war remains.

Appendix: The Impact of Oil on the World Economy Comparison of 1973-1974 with 1979-1980

SIMILARITIES

Oil Price Rises

i) The major oil price rises took place in several steps both in 1973 (October and December) and in 1979 (most importantly July and December–January 1980).

ii) The size of the oil price shock was roughly of the same magnitude, representing 2 per cent of OECD area GNP.

Fiscal Policy

Mildly restrictive in 1973–1974; moderately restrictive in 1979, with a tendency towards tightening in 1979 and early 1980.

Monetary Policy

Successive tightening during 1974 and the second half of 1979 and early 1980.

Conjunctural State

The OECD economy was booming in the first half of 1973, with a peak GNP growth rate of 8½ per cent for the major seven countries, and decelerated in the second half of the year. In the first half of 1979 before the major oil price rise of July, GNP was already decelerating in the OECD area although not from such a high rate.

Source: OECD, *Economic Outlook*, no. 27 (July 1980).

DIFFERENCES

Those two major oil price rises translated into a 350 per cent rise in imported oil prices in 1973–1974 and a rise of about 130 per cent in imported oil prices in the period from the end of 1978 to the middle of 1980.

Policy was relaxed in 1975, whereas it appears as if policy may remain tight at a similar stage in the second period of 'oil shock'.

Given the widespread adoption of monetary targets over recent years and the concern about excessive exchange rate fluctuations, this tightening seems to be less abrupt and better balanced than in 1973–1974 without accommodating the acceleration of domestic inflation; and monetary policies seem to be more convergent. Real M2 for the major seven countries actually fell throughout 1974 (−4½ per cent between the fourth quarters of 1973 and 1974), while it started falling only in the fourth quarter of 1979.

(continued)

Use of Public Power

SIMILARITIES

Capacity Utilisation

Capacity utilisation rates rose strongly during 1973 (peaking towards the end of the year in most major countries). Rates were also rising in 1979 in most countries, although not in the United States.

Synchronisation

Inflation

Corporate Financial Position

Current Balances

The swing of the OECD area current balance between 1978 and 1980 relative to GNP is expected to be almost identical to that recorded between 1972 and 1974 (1½ per cent of area GNP).

5. *Effective Policy-Making*

Object: to specify a scale of success or failure of government action conditional on (and made more effective by) the efficient negotiation of policy between organized interest groups.

The tentative criteria – intended to measure the benefits and the cost of different national policies (long- and short-term); prices; employment; exchange rates and current account balance of payments; investment – mainly in physical terms, but also in human and social capital.

The general conclusion: some nations – outstandingly Japan, but also in great measure Germany and a number of the smaller democracies of Western Europe – had come through the 1970s with very little pain. They had managed their affairs in conditions of relatively modest inflation, contained unemployment, and little loss of social welfare; even the personal incomes continued to grow. The strategies of the successful and the less successful countries are subjected to fuller analysis in the following four chapters.

6. *Changing Character of Planning; Indicative and Imperative Planning in France, Crypto-planning in Germany.*[3]

Planning in the 1970s meant making market forces more efficacious. Planning as device for identifying long-term risks and thus reducing entrepreneurial uncertainties. Some new problems were energy and the environment (social costs pinned increasingly on entrepreneurs). Capital costs are on the increase. Labour costs acquire some of the character of capital commitment, as element of risk in hiring increases. There is therefore more need for incentives from public authorities. Increased public expenditures, typically with long lead time, need to be planned in the context of a well-defined public policy system.

DIFFERENCES

But i) they have been slowly and steadily rising from the low levels in 1975, maybe reflecting the tendency of business to direct investment away from that increasing capacity, whereas before 1973 capacity utilisation rates had been more cyclical; ii) at the 1973 cyclical peak, there were shortages of capacity in major materials industries rather than in the manufacturing sector as a whole. No such evidence this time.

In the period from end-1971 to mid-1973 all of the major OECD countries experienced a strong upswing (see *Economic Outlook* 14, Chart B, page 24). In 1979, by contrast, de-synchronisation prevailed, with considerable buoyancy in Japan and Germany, a weakening of demand in the United States and an intermediate position in many other countries.

Although the oil price shock is similar in both cases, inflation is lower in the second half of 1979 and the first half of 1980 than in both half-years of 1974, mainly because of unit labour costs, which seem to be growing more modestly this time. Furthermore, inflation reacted more strongly in 1973–1974 when the spread of private consumption deflator growth rates more than doubled between the second half of 1973 and the first half of 1974, while it is likely to increase by about a third on this occasion (see also Chart B).

The financial situation of enterprises in the second half of 1979 appears healthier than in the first half of 1974 (balance sheets have been restructured, debt maturities lengthened, liquidity and self-financing ratios improved).

The pattern of current balances among OECD countries may be more sustainable than that which emerged after the first oil crisis.

The Argument Continued

**Outline of the rest of the book
as planned by Andrew Shonfield**

The purpose of this section is to carry on the argument, in the broadest terms, beyond the point at which the author's definite draft of the book was interrupted. The notes that follow have been selected from his working papers and are arranged in chapter form, from 4 to 13. In the original design, '4: The Backlash against Government Intervention' followed on the text of Chapters 1 to 3 of the present book and was intended to complete the first section of the entire scheme, under the general heading of 'The Changed Economic Context – 1960s and 1970s'. Certain implications of the backlash have been summarized earlier in this book, in the Introduction, pp. xvii–xx, and are not repeated here.

4. The Backlash Against Government Intervention

The scope of public authority in economic and social affairs is enlarged while changing attitudes, including 'anti-government backlash', limit, in varying degrees, its substantial power.

The backlash has a variety of aspects, such as a growing impatience with too much nannying, too little personal choice; the re-

jection of too much regulation, reputed to paralyse entrepreneurial impulses; the rebellion about public expenditure which grew too fast and had insufficient returns on high investment. In spite of rising public expenditure, the redistribution of income does not fulfil objectives of equality. However, the welfare umbrella now extends over wider sections of the population.

Is there a crisis in the welfare system itself? Among the many misconceptions about its working are the following:

– that we have already redistributed incomes sufficiently. Not true; cf. OECD figures[1] which show that welfare has been about the *inclusion* of previously excluded groups, about '*democratization*', rather than about achieving equality.
– that all fully-industrialized Western-style nations now have uniformly high welfare standards. Not true of laggards, such as the UK and, particularly, Japan.
– that an increasingly high proportion of the national product is being spent on welfare. Not true generally –see p. xix above and n. 7, p. 117.

Do the citizens of high welfare societies want to opt out of publicly provided welfare schemes – and pay less tax, and have more personal choice? In Europe there is no going back on the desire for security – in old age, in sickness, in unemployment. There is some evidence (from German surveys) that there is no appreciable difference between the welfare demanded by the proletarians and by the middle classes. Nevertheless, as proletarians become *embourgeoisé,* they often reject the State as protector. In the UK they want not less welfare service but more *choice* – through private schemes, such as commercial personal insurance (despite its many snags). Is the US experience relevant? Proposition 13 *was* preeminently about economics – but some of its proponents were trying to shift responsibility from local and state level to central government level.

Reagan's policy is not particularly against *welfare,* but rather an attempt to cut *most* public expenditure. Will he succeed? Not so long ago, in 1979, US public opinion was against such a reduction.[2]

Does planning of the new type have to be *comprehensive?* No
– only it should be *wide-ranging* enough to identify possible mis-
matches of resources, especially in timing of complementary enterprises.

French transparency in planning

In France the scope of direct government intervention was on the
increase after 1975. Earlier it appeared to be decreasing: it had by
degrees become limited to research and development assistance
(which did not on the whole discriminate between branches of the
economy); to fiscal encouragement of industrial investment generally; and to some discreet corporate structure adjustment,
designed to produce enterprises of the right size to invest and
export.

How was it that this relatively low degree of policy intervention
seemingly helped France to a shallower recession in 1974/5 than
that which hit other EEC countries, including Germany? To what
extent were the monetary and fiscal policies more accommodating
than elsewhere? How important was the fact that the labour market functioned efficiently (in contrast with that of Germany)
against a background of weak trade unions?

Post-1975, the *Programmes d'Action Prioritaire* emphasized investment subsidies intended to counteract, for counter-cyclical
purposes, the deficiencies of private demand. The *Grandes Entre-
prises Nationales* were largely used as instruments in the process,
the nationalized sector absorbing 60 per cent of the total increase
in productive investment. Activity was sustained; the balance of
payments recovered into surplus as against the German deficit from
1979 onwards. But at the end of the 1970s unemployment and
inflation were higher than in Germany.

Planning, German style

In theory, a horror of centralized power over the economy and of
long-term planning; but the Germans have increasingly been driven into it. Some features: sectoral planning, e.g. in education and
in transport; co-ordination of quasi-independent *Länder* into federal structure; growth of social welfare, and fear of its inflationary
effects; discovery that fiscal planning requires taking a view on the
behaviour of economic variables as a whole.

Very extensive system of monitoring has developed since 1967. After the 'social disaster' of the 1974 *Beamtenstreik,* proposals for intervention come with increasing urgency, if the variables deviate much from the desirable long-term objectives and the path leading to them.

In spite of the unofficial bargain with trade unions in the autumn of 1974 – when a figure for the rise in the money supply was agreed on assumptions about wages, made in agreement with the unions – both they and the Bundesbank cling to the myth of free bargaining.

The government is driven to adopt long/medium-term employment targets as part of the unofficial incomes policy deal. German economic policy thinking in the late 1970s emphasizes increasingly the need for policies directed towards the supply side of the economy, away from demand management.

On micro-intervention: An important difference between the French and the German style is that French officials have the *habit* of intervention and discrimination at the level of the individual firm; 'structural policy' includes the business of putting individual enterprises into fresh shapes, by mergers etc. The Germans are more inhibited, though they do constantly intervene.

7. Japan, a Phenomenon on its Own?

Japan was probably the most successful country in dealing with the impact of business fluctuations. Most advanced corporatism.

The Japanese authorities (to a degree unusual among Western countries) have been able to combine 'fine tuning' of the economy with a high, sustained rate of growth. This is because the Japanese economy has been exceptionally responsive to *short-term* shifts in credit policy – while retaining its confidence that credit would accommodate itself to the needs of *long-term* expansion, as soon as the central bank was satisfied that the twin objectives, balance of payments and relatively stable prices, had been attained. The Tokyo authorities just seem to be that much more effective than their counterparts in Europe and America in persuading businessmen to behave in the desirable ways.

In the early 1980s Japan faces major problems of structural adjustment, higher unemployment, lower profits, in a number of industries which have absorbed immense resources. There have been signs that the old-style system of guidance of investment from the centre (e.g. through MITI) is breaking down, in part at least because of the internationalization of financial resources, but in large measure because of a deliberate government preference for an effectively functioning market system. However, while long-term planning forecasts are under suspicion, administrative guidance is still very much a factor in the thinking of the big companies.

If Japanese planning works, it is in the favourable context of a highly flexible labour price (approximating to Hayek's ideal, though, paradoxically, within the setting of a planned economy which he dismisses as a chimera). However, some big structural changes are in the air which may affect the wage structure and the labour markets in general – for example, the whole issue of moving social welfare over from the big corporations to the public sector. Would a normally functioning state welfare system destroy the dual structure of the economy, in the sense that there would no longer be the intensive competition for jobs in the large companies?

To what extent will the Japanese system of labour relations withstand the new pressures? Will unions remain weak and non militant in conditions of lower growth, when they can no longer ride on the prosperity of the big corporations, where wages have in the past been on average an estimated 40 per cent higher than in the rest of the economy? As the high-wage, high-productivity, 'life-time' employment sector diminishes in importance, how will the economy adapt to the increased emphasis on the tertiary sector, with its low productivity growth?

8. Have the Smaller Democracies Got Better Solutions?

Are there some general lessons to be learnt from the experience of the Scandinavian nations, and also from countries like the Netherlands and Austria? Has the social democratic dominance in their political thinking been decisive, especially in the way they tackled the 1970s business cycles? What gave these countries their seeming advantage? A number of answers suggest themselves – greater social cohesion, together with well-developed techniques of securing public assent (and incidental confidence in government); or the readier access to the international capital market – for relatively small sums; or again, more skill and practice in adapting industrial structures to changes in foreign trade patterns; or a combination of all these sets of factors. Or perhaps the advantage is spurious, only one of delayed effects of the business cycle? These smaller democracies continued to go for high growth in the mid-1970s slump (while others deflated). In the process some ran heavy balance of payments deficits; Denmark, however, was able to combine this with membership of the 'Snake'. Then, from late 1977 onwards, they were belatedly forced to adjust, but did so at a deliberate pace, minimizing the effects on employment.

Sweden appears to have practised 'fine tuning' with considerable success, including in the most difficult 1974/5 period. The Netherlands and Austria, too, seem to have had some success with 'fine tuning'. Yet these are countries most especially vulnerable to the uncontrollable influences from external trade and finance. In spite of their dependence on foreign trade, they acted as if they had more autonomy, and they took bigger risks, than the large nations.

The important difference may be between nations who recognize that they *are* 'small countries', and adapt their policies accordingly, and those who have been slow in recognizing that a population of fifty million or so is no key to 'large country' status. In Europe, EEC formal obligations have helped to make some of the bigger countries begin to act *as if* they were small. However, France and the UK show a special resistance to this recognition of diminished status.

9. *'Non-intervention' in the USA and the UK*

The *USA* in the 1964–74 period was a dynamic, innovative society, accomplishing the remarkable feat of integrating minority and other 'out' groups in the name of the 'Great Society'. The economic basis for the pervasive spirit of innovation rested on the immense fiscal capacity of the American economy. Mid-1970s informed commentators,[4] while recognizing the short-term obstacles to accommodating new burdens on the budget, saw it as being 'much more amenable to policy changes' in the long run. Reflecting in 1974 on the decade just ended, they were encouraged to observe that large cuts in personal and corporate tax rates were accommodated during the years when the country was affording the long and costly Vietnam War, as well as several major social reform programmes.

Growth of executive power, which showed up clearly in the 'imperial presidency' of Richard Nixon, was a process which began much earlier; marked effect – sometimes benign – during the Kennedy and Johnson presidencies, allowing the President to by-pass Congressional prejudices in pursuit of liberal reform: e.g. Kennedy's decree denying Federal funds to any housing projects which admitted racial discrimination; Johnson denying government contracts to businesses practising sex discrimination in employment. It was the growth in the scale of government intervention in the economy which had made such pressures possible: hardly any housing scheme not involving Federal funding; hardly any big firms not dependent on some Federal contracts.

The changed context of the later 1970s; two notable features: First, US productivity growth slowed down very markedly – an *extreme* of a general trend. The striking aspect of this was that the downward trend from the already relatively low growth levels of the 1960s appeared to be reinforced by the boom of 1976/9. In the second place, household savings as a proportion of disposable income – rather low to begin with – fell dramatically at the end of the 1970s (a novel assertion, perhaps, of rational consumer behaviour in the face of inflation?).

Disappointment with US economic performance reinforced the already vigorous non-interventionist mood generated by the pro-market school of economists from the 1960s onwards; it found a ready sounding board in the rhetoric of the new Republican Administration. Among the questions to be asked about Reagan's programme:

- To what extent will the demands from industry for less interference with market processes have to be met by concessions which themselves require interventionist legislation?
- In what measure will the built-in tendency of the US economy towards high cyclical unemployment restrict the policy-makers' room to manoeuvre in the execution of monetarist policies?
- Will the scale of government intervention in the economy be materially reduced in areas in which organized pressure groups – consumers, environmentalists, ethnic minorities, the disadvantaged – have in the past stimulated reform programmes?
- Starting from Carter's election in 1976, American policies, intended to stimulate domestic expansion, were being conducted as if external constraints on the US economy were relatively insignificant. To what extent will the Reagan Administration compensate for this misconception?
- Which of the judicial processes established to control the pressures of executive power on the economy will be regarded as otiose?

In the *United Kingdom,* the mixed economy has certainly been disappointing: it must be seen as an extreme example of the failure of public policy – failure to reach common European standards of economic growth and welfare. The elements in this depressing economic scene: weak private initiative; strong privately organized pressure groups; a government which, in its attempt to achieve a total break with Keynesianism, rejects the charitable and supervisory role of the State, preferring a determined pro-market stance.

However, it finds it 'difficult to bring about a significant change in the ratio between publicly-owned and private assets. . . .'[5] As in America, non-interventionist rhetoric prevails. In spite of it, industrial lame ducks continue to be supported. North Sea oil, a potential buffer against external shocks, is used inadequately. How would a government accustomed to wholehearted planning, such as the French, have used the oil resource? In the short term: to give its economy more *national autonomy;* to take more risks with *investment;* to raise *employment.* In the long-term: to pursue vigorously the objective of *raising productivity;* to *reduce* decisively the *taxes* which inhibit capital investment.

The Thatcher Government's monetary extremism has led to measures which are made to bear too heavy a load of economic policy at large, and are used as a *substitute* for other actions, e.g. in the field of fiscal policy, which ought to have complemented monetary policy – all this at a time when the Government was undertaking a deliberate upheaval in the arrangements governing taxation, foreign exchange controls, wages and incomes policies, and so on. The incompatibility between the use of market mechanisms and planning, which the Thatcher Government emphasized to an exaggerated degree, is in any case based on false premises: discovering the limits of the capacity for short-term intervention does not imply the withdrawal of public direction in the long term.

There were, as of December 1980, no signs of readiness on the part of the British (any more than there are on the part of the new Republican Administration in the USA) to modify in any way the rigours of their monetary policies for reasons connected with international objectives.

There is little sign of a recognition of the need for modern-style incomes policies, not necessarily explicitly committed to a particular figure. Here the more successful nations such as the Germans and the Japanese should serve as an example, in their insistence on the flexibility of the response by the workers to business conditions and profit opportunities.

Is the UK in a situation of suppressed civil war? No, but there is a seemingly insoluble mystery about the failure of the modern British work ethic to respond to crises. There is a danger of official trade unions becoming non-viable. A particular difference between present-day UK and France: the French appeared to proceed from the consciousness that insurrection is within the realm of possibility; the Thatcher Government seemed to go on as if there were no possibility of violent opposition to the effects of Tory policies.

10. International Dimensions

We have come to depend for our prosperity on a set of arrangements which keep international trade routes open – and we must, if possible, maintain the momentum of the last twenty-five years to open them further. If there is one thing that we know we cannot afford it is trade wars.

The internationalization of large-scale business enterprise, most especially American enterprise, is one of the familiar facts of corporate developments since the early 1960s. How has this affected the structure of decision-making within the typical large corporation? There is considerable evidence that the great multinational enterprises changed their character in the mid-1960s, ceasing to concern themselves exclusively with the serving of local markets by local production and becoming more truly international in the style of their management decisions. The implications of such a change for the relationship between large corporate enterprises and the national governments of host countries need to be explored.

The internationalization of production has been accompanied during the 1960s and 1970s by a remarkable revival of international capital markets. Moreover, governments, while being irked on occasion by the independent power of these markets, have engaged in a kind of tacit compact to abstain from any serious effort at controlling them. This refers in particular to the Eurocurrency market, which has become especially supplied with funds, including latterly the oil producers' surpluses. Governments of advanced industrial countries have come to depend on it (to a degree which is highly unusual by historical standards) to sustain their currencies during periods of balance of payments trouble.

An accompanying feature is a marked acceleration in the tempo of consultation between nations for purposes of economic policy-making. That in turn makes the structure of low-tariff, unrestricted trading, established in the 1950s and 1960s, more robust. Less recourse to violent measures, which can in time become sustained, such as import controls. (Import deposits are thought of as a temporary expedient.)

In consequence, governments are more constrained by the views of the private market operators (lenders) about the appropriate economic policy. The *private* operators in turn are increasingly influenced by IMF (*public*) as lenders of last resort. For instance, the UK in the mid-1970s was under pressure to cut its public deficit by more than it would have wished in order to impress the IMF and more conservatively inclined foreign governments, because these in turn provide a kind of *placet* for the market.

The effect in this case was to tighten international controls over an errant national government. The consequence is to make a medium-to-big country, say Britain or France, much more like a small country in its international economic relations and in how it responds to international pressures in conditions of weakness.

On the other hand, small countries with a good economic track record, like Sweden, can use the international capital market to support them while they go ahead with some original economic experiments (e.g. anticyclical policy of Sweden in 1975 and its high balance-of-payments deficit aftermath; policy for slow elimination of deficit and maintenance of high employment in the late 1970s). All this indicates a degree of liberation of small countries from the constraints operated on them pre-war by the great powers.

Comeback of *central banks* in international relations. They are the natural agents of policy in a sphere where money-market factors have been greatly reinforced. The 'money market' being outstandingly a market in which leadership by the big buyers/sellers, the commercial banks and the major financial institutions, is predominant: these are the firms which in the national context are in a close symbiotic relationship with the central banks. There are typically only three to four such banks in the medium-sized countries and up to ten in the US; it is a very tight community.

The fact that the more independent central banks in the powerful countries, Germany and the USA, *are* more independent, reinforces the suppressed impulse of the central banks of the UK and France (which are subject to strong Treasury tutelage) to demand more independence. The 'Basle Effect' – strong central banks propping up the weak. This has a certain feedback into domestic economic policy, especially when the determination of monetary aggregates becomes so prominent in policy-making (cf. struggle between the Federal Reserve and the Carter Administration).

11. The New Corporatism

Capacity and limitations of organizations in the private sector to respond to the requirements of structural change, with special emphasis on the corporatist (versus 'market') formula for the management of the economy. The corporatist mode of making public policy, while inevitable, is commonly –though not invariably – benign.

Corporatism as a means of preserving *pluralism* in a democracy. The expression of public interest depends on the insistent voices of a growing number of pressure groups: organized labour, big business, anti-trust lobbies, consumer movements, the ecology lobby, ethnic minorities, women, the old, the disadvantaged.

What does efficient corporatism depend on in a democratic society? The 'corporations' must have legitimacy, transparency, accountability to public authority, and a considerable measure of control over their members. They must be integrated into the process of policy-making at national/international levels. These requirements distinguish legitimate democratic corporatism from legitimized factionalism.

How to measure the *efficiency* of corporatism? E.g. by its capacity to restrain inflationary forces in the 1970s. Any attempt to put the results on a *scale of relative efficiency* cannot leave out of account other variables, such as the skill and power of governmental policymaking; the particular stage of the business cycle which is the starting point; the influence of labour market forces.

Attitudes to 'corporations' differ markedly between countries. In Sweden and Denmark the system is under some strain but they have on the whole been part of the success of the smaller democracies, Austria being the outstanding case. In these small countries such 'corporations' *are* the government. However, parliamentary government is not thereby rendered ineffectual: it is false to see parliament and 'corporations' as rivals. They are not external to government as such. The British way of classifying institutions suffers from too sharp a distinction between *public* bodies – accountable, and *private* ones – not accountable. One of the problems in the UK is the restrictive notion of *public law,* which excludes e.g. trade unions. Trade unions *are* public law bodies, and need to be made more transparent.

In the USA there is a current notion that smaller interest groups and special claimants will tend to win out against governments – public authorities purporting to represent the mass of consumers and tax payers. This has led in the past to the belief that the *only* way to secure the *public interest* is to enforce resistance to the

demands of special interest groups by a constitutional limitation
on the financial responsiveness of governments. Measures of active
de-regulation will be the chosen tool of the new Republican Administration.

What is required for the sake of the majority, not fully represented by any pressure group, is more effective surveillance of the
coalition between government and its corporatist partners, primarily by means of new judicial institutions, but also by parliament. The need to develop and preserve public institutions over
which the direct influence of voters is limited (e.g. central banks;
international institutions).

12. The Mixed Economy for the 1980s

The particular phobias in the UK about the mixed economy:

After the 'commanding heights' rhetoric of the Left, coupled with
weak Labour leadership, and the large (and unhappy) role played
by public enterprise investments in the National Plan of the 1960s,
comes the ferocious Tory anti-planning, anti-public enterprise
ethos. Outside the UK, however, the Right does not treat nationalized industry policy as a *major* ideological issue. Conversely, in
France the Left is not necessarily 'anti-market' and in Italy the
communists are very wary of nationalization as a soft option.

British public enterprise becomes less like private enterprise, because of powerful ministerial control, *inhibiting entrepreneurship*.
The weakness of public enterprises (which is by no means uniform) is a symptom of the general weakness and low profitability
of British industry.

There may also be a problem of guaranteeing the national attachment of companies in an increasingly international corporate
world. If a government holds part of the equity of an enterprise
with international dimensions, is this enough to make the national
voice clearly heard in the company's policy-making?

In general, governments are less assured and active, having re-
cently made notably wrong medium/long-term predictions of output, growth, etc.; in the second half of the 1970s they were loath
to take on increased financial and *directional* responsibilities.

There is a distinct preference for spreading investment risks through decentralization of capital spending decisions; in effect less intervention, because there is more uncertainty – just when the very uncertainty tends to reduce investment and when more investment is required to speed structural changes. In any case, the extremely rapid expansion of public spending from the mid-1960s on, continuing with the business cycle of the 1970s, has caused uneasiness about the balance of public and private power, and also about the omnicompetence of the State.

One of the chief constraints on economic policy-making in the early 1980s is the disparity between the investment needs for structural change, and the funds likely to be made available by private investors. Money is more expensive; bankers, faced with a higher business failure rate, become less venturesome; public authorities tend to squeeze banks (e.g. by raising reserve ratios, imposing tougher conditions for acting as lender of last resort) in pursuit of disinflationary policies.

The upshot is that smaller firms are deterred from engaging in big bold investments. Bigger firms are often saddled with existing stock of less efficient capital which they can only write off gradually, and delay or slow down new investment until they have done so. Because of the slowdown and changes in the structure of the economy, a higher proportion of investment has a longer lead time. To invest in these circumstances implies a willingness to accept a higher level of indebtedness (and/or a longer period of indebtedness), or a lower rate of return on existing capital assets.

Uncertainty about future interest rates, as well as the high level of rates at present, in any case inhibits productive investment. New financial technologies are helping to diminish this influence – earnings and interest rates are being increasingly tailor-made to meet potential lenders' needs (e.g. 'floating rate bonds'). But the fact that political considerations (including anti-inflation tactics) enter largely into exchange-parity plus interest-rate decisions means that in future additional inputs by the State – such as political safeguards and cheap insurance against increased uncertainty – are needed. All this tends to make increased demands on the State, just at a time when it is trying to reduce its active, financial and regulatory, role in the economic system.

To meet problems arising out of the reduced marginal efficiency and greater cost of capital (because of high interest rates, expectations of slower growth, and the higher risks implied in great measure by these very causes), the investment needs require mainly publicly-provided finance, uninhibited centralized decision-making and good timing.

The ethos of private enterprise in the conduct of its relationships with public authority is changing. There is an apparent increase in the dependence of private corporate enterprises, especially when they are involved in large-scale investment decisions, on the approval and support of governments. The old oppositional spirit, which was characteristic especially of some big American corporations, seems to be markedly less in evidence. Yet there are some notable respects in which the effective power of corporate enterprise has been enlarged. Perhaps the answer to the riddle presented by the taming of the aggressive sentiment, characteristic of the old style of business enterprise, lies in the habit-forming practice of profitable collaboration with government and para-governmental institutions in one or other of their many manifestations.

13. Conclusion: The Tolerant Society and the Assertion of Social Authority

Andrew Shonfield sketched out the final chapter of the book at the end of 1980. Much of the draft revolves round the discussion of ideas contained in Lester Thurow's Zero-Sum Society,[6] and a critique of the political thought of Milton Friedman (together with E. J. Mishan's anti-Friedmanite commentary). However, he also returned to a central theme of his thinking – the idea of a historical cycle of the assertion of authoritarianism following on periods of marked permissiveness. His discussion of such a cycle has been summarized in what follows.

Looking back over the fifteen years since the mid-1960s, such economic doctrines as monetarism, central bank power, and fiscal conservatism have not provided keys to *ideal policies*. The positive experience of the small democracies contradicted the first two doctrines; that of Japan, the last. What mattered decisively was the *efficiency of institutional instruments* – those used for the consensus management of labour conflict, and also the ones which eased the path to innovation (as in Germany and Japan).

Perhaps the most important questions about the 1980s are to do with the future of the social democracies. Has the need to assert greater authority from the centre (in the form of the measures taken post-1973) eroded them? Will the democratic nations of the 1980s turn out to be ungovernable? Theories of ungovernability seem peculiarly relevant to the political conditions which, in the age of 'single-issue' interest groups, make effective government exceptionally difficult.

Examining the relatively recent past for historical analogues of minority-group pressures for which the European political system failed to provide adequate accommodation, we find two such great forces (through the writings of the French historian, Élie Halévy; cf. his essay on the origins of the First World War, 'The World Crisis of 1914–1918').[7] Both gathered strength from the late nineteenth century onwards, and markedly in the 1900s. One was the assertion of rights of national minorities; the other, the claims of organized labour for political and economic power either through a workers' socialist party, or through syndicalist action. Is it possible to identify similar forces at work in the years since the end of the Second World War? Is it plausible, for example, to argue that the issue of national minorities before the First World War bears a close resemblance to that of social heterogeneity in the second half of the twentieth century? The rights of the first were denied almost in their entirety by authoritarian regimes, totally conformist in spirit; homogeneity enhanced the collective will. The political mood prevailing since 1945 is the opposite of this; collective strength derives from social structures which accommodate diversity.

As to the second great force of the earlier period: in the pre-1914 bourgeois-dominated society the most prominent disadvantaged group consisted of propertyless manual labourers. Slowly the legitimacy of their organizations and their claims to some political power were recognized. The process was reversed for a time by the authoritarian regimes in the 1930s. There was no room to accommodate alternative sources of power in societies ruled by totalitarian parties acting in the name of the overwhelming majority.

On the face of it, the disadvantaged groups, whose welfare has been the objective of social reform since the end of the Second World War, would be much more vulnerable to authoritarian majority rule than the trade unions had been. The trade unions were after all sustained by their own people and funds; they demanded, and achieved, legitimacy. Their leaders claim to represent majorities of workers in different trades and they make bargains which often set legal standards. They can, and do, practise the tyranny of majority rule.

The disadvantaged groups which have had the attention of the post-war welfare state have in general no capacity for mobilization equal to or approaching that of trade unionists. Lester Thurow's argument that, in future, major economic adjustment cannot take place without the active assent of these groups – which in the past have been the voiceless victims of economic change – may be mistaken. If the mood of the majority changed, came to be dominated by the need to defend its existing gains, there would be no difficulty in finding satisfying formulas to justify the erosion of the welfare of weakly organized minorities.

Will societies remain so committed to 'openness' and tolerance of the foreigner when international interdependence, in the shape of international trade as a proportion of *total* transactions, ceases to grow at the rapid rate of 1945–75? If international trade becomes not an engine of economic growth but a threatening constraint on it (as in the 1930s), many things will go by the board. This emphasizes the importance of giving, throughout the OECD, the greatest degree of priority to matters of international industrial policy in order to maintain the 'openness' gained since 1945.

Notes

Full titles and publication details of books and articles are given once only; subsequent references are in abbreviated form.

Notes to Introduction (pp. xiii—xxiv)

1. Andrew Shonfield, 'The Politics of the Mixed Economy in the International System of the 1970s', *International Affairs,* vol. 56, no. 1 (Jan. 1980), London, p. 1.
2. Charles P. Kindleberger, 'The Best Laid Plans', *Challenge* (May–June 1966), White Plains, NY.
3. *British Economic Policy since the War,* Penguin, Harmondsworth (1958), p. 215.
4. Bernard Cazes, 'L'Etat-protecteur est il allé trop loin?', mimeo discussion paper (1977); 'L'état-protecteur contraint à une double manoeuvre', *Futuribles,* no. 40 (Jan. 1981).
5. OECD, *Public Expenditure Trends* (1978), Table 2, p. 14.
6. ibid. p. 15.
7. For the decrease in *real terms* of the share of GDP taken up by public spending in general in a variety of OECD countries, see Hugh Heclo's mimeo paper, 'Public Expenditure in Sweden, prepared for the Conference on Political Liberty and Collective Welfare', Bonn, West Germany (December 1976), Table 13, p. 31. Heclo bases his table on calculations by Morris Beck, published in the *National Tax Journal* in March 1976.
8. Andrew Shonfield, Chatham House Lecture, 'The future of capitalism after the world slump of the 1970s', Guildhall, London (16 Feb. 1977).
9. In a personal letter to Paolo Baffi, former head of the Banca d'Italia, 3 Sept. 1980.

10. Andrew Shonfield, 'Western Capitalism: A New Balance between Private and Public Power?', *Executive*, vol. 4, no. 2 (March 1978), Cornell, p. 38.

Notes to Chapter 1 (pp. 3-36)

1. NIESR, *Economic Review*, July 1961, 'Economic Growth: The last hundred years', by D. C. Paige, E. T. Blackaby, S. Freund, p. 37. See Table 6, p. 36, which puts the story of the 1950s into the context of longer periods of economic growth, up to the First World War and subsequent to it. The speed-up of the fifties could be regarded as the belated response of a system which during most of the twentieth century had been performing below par. The authors pointed to a number of new forces, apparent by the end of the 1950s, which they thought *might* sustain economic growth at a level above the historic average — notably the development of techniques of planning in the context of free enterprise economies; the avoidance of serious business-cycle downturns; and the process of West European economic integration.

2. Peter F. Drucker, *The Age of Discontinuity*, Heinemann, London 1969, pp. 4 ff. *Editorial note:* An additional (manuscript) note by Andrew Shonfield is relevant here; it emphasizes that Drucker *did* believe in *discontinuities* as well as continuity, but different ones from those discussed in the present book.

3. ibid. p. 4.

4. The United States, whose productive performance was, as noted, exceptionally good in the years preceding the First World War – annual industrial output increased much faster than that of the major European industrial nations – tends to bias the long-term picture. Because of this exceptional performance, it would necessarily take the United States longer, if it maintained the average Western growth rate, than other countries to get back on to its earlier trend line. The aggregate result for the Western industrial world as a whole is strongly influenced by this because the United States makes up such a large proportion of its total output – around 40 per cent during the period under consideration. Since US economic growth after the Second World War was in fact relatively slow compared with that of the other industrial countries, the time taken to reach the point where the level of its output had risen sufficiently to intersect the long-term trend-line was further extended. Peter Drucker's picture of long-term continuity (which he extends beyond 1960) is accordingly overwhelmingly influenced by the particular circumstances of the United

States. For a comprehensive analysis of the comparative data on the industrial performance of the US with that of other leading countries before the First World War, see W. A. Lewis, *Growth and Fluctuations, 1870–1913,* Allen & Unwin, London 1978, especially Appendix II.

5. See OECD, *Manpower and Employment: Problems and Prospects,* Paris 1978, Table 5, p. 41.

6. For a comparison of the growth rates in seven industrial countries, 1950–77, see E. F. Denison, *Accounting for Slower Economic Growth – The United States in the 1970s,* Brookings, Washington 1979, Table 9-2, p. 146. Angus Maddison's 'Long Run Dynamics of Productivity Growth', in the *Banca Nazionale del Lavoro Quarterly Review* no. 128 (March 1979), Rome, Table 2, p. 4, shows levels of productivity in 1950 and in 1977 for a wider selection of industrial countries.

7. See E. F. Denison, *Accounting for US Economic Growth, 1929–1969,* Brookings, Washington 1974. Table 2-2, p. 13, shows that in the period 1965–9 employment rose at double the rate of the previous five years, while national income per person employed rose by under half of the previous rate of increase.

8. ibid. p. 120.

9. See OECD, *Manpower and Employment,* Table 4, p. 38.

10. See CEC, *Sectoral Change in the European Economies from 1960 to the Recession,* Brussels 1978, Table 1, p. 64, from which this figure and other data on employment in the text are derived. The figures refer to the six largest Community countries, France, Germany, United Kingdom, Italy, Netherlands, and Belgium, where total employment amounted to around 100 million at the beginning of the 1970s.

11. Within the EEC, railway employment went down by more than a quarter from a little over 1.6 m. to just about 1.2 m. between 1960 and 1973.

    The figure embraces an actual *increase* in the number employed on the railways in Italy of about 17 per cent. Otherwise, the downward trend was general; in the United Kingdom it was much more marked (and earlier) than elsewhere, with a reduction of nearly two-thirds. Estimates based on data from *Annual Bulletin of Transport Statistics for Europe,* 1963 and 1973.

12. A. Lindbeck, *Swedish Economic Policy,* Macmillan, London 1975, p. 157.

13. CEC, *Sectoral Change in the European Economies,* p. 9.

14. F. A. Hayek, *Studies in Philosophy, Politics and Economics,* Routledge, London 1967, p. 275.

15. ibid. p. 275.
16. OECD, *The Impact of the Newly Industrializing Countries on Production and Trade in Manufactures*, Paris 1979, p. 42. See also, for further evidence on changes in employment structure before 1970, p. 44, footnote 19. The NICs under study consist of four south European countries: Spain, Portugal, Greece, Yugoslavia; four Asian countries: Hong Kong, Korea, Taiwan, Singapore; Brazil and Mexico are also included.
17. ibid., especially Table 1, p. 18. See also IBRD, *World Development Report*, Washington 1978, and a comprehensive statement by Fred Bergsten, US Assistant Secretary of the Treasury, before the Conference Board, New York, on 5 June 1978; and see his 'The US Trade Balance and American Competitiveness Revisited', p. 113, in *International Economic Policy of the United States: Selected Papers, 1977–1979*, Lexington Books, Lexington, Mass., 1980.
18. OECD, *The Impact of the Newly Industrializing Countries*, p. 33.
19. Deutsches Institut für Wirtschaftsforschung, *Wochenbericht* 15/78, Berlin, 13 April 1978, p. 149.
20. OECD, *Economic Outlook*, no. 23 (1978), p. 10.
21. An agreement of some fifty GATT member-countries, superseding 1960s arrangements for control of world trade in cotton textiles; it was first concluded on 20 December 1973, and came into effect on 1 January 1974, to run for four years. The MFA, which also established a permanent Textile Surveillance Body and a Textiles Committee within the GATT, covers most wool, cotton, and man-made fibres, as well as piece-goods and made-up articles made of such fibres. It seeks to keep the level of barriers against textile imports from whatever source as low as possible and to control those restraints which are essential to avoid disruption of the domestic textile industries of member countries. At the same time, the MFA aims at ensuring that textile exports from developing countries are assured an increasing share of world markets, while seeking to minimize the disruptive effect of such expansion.

     The Arrangement was extended for another four years, until 31 December 1981, by a protocol agreed on 14 December 1977, and again, in a modified form, at the end of 1981.
22. See, e.g., two articles by C. Fred Bergsten, 'The Threat from the Third World' and 'The Threat is Real', *Foreign Policy*, New York, nos. 11 (1973) and 14 (1974).
23. OECD, *Economic Outlook*, no. 23 (1978), p. xii.
24. For a discussion of this issue see Andrew Shonfield's essay in the

book he edited on *International Economic Relations 1958–1971*, Oxford University Press 1976, vol. 1, part I, chapter 5.

25. A. Maizels, *Industrial Growth and World Trade*, Cambridge University Press 1963, pp. 79 ff.
26. ibid.
27. W. A. Lewis, *Growth and Fluctuations*, pp. 169 ff.
28. ibid. p. 176.
29. GATT, *International Trade 1979/80*, Geneva 1980.
30. France alone was at that stage an exception.
31. OECD, *Interfutures* Report, *Facing the Future*, Paris 1979, p. 186.
32. In A. G. Heidenheimer, H. Heclo, C. T. Adams, *Comparative Public Policy: the Politics of Social Choice in Europe and America*, Macmillan, London 1976, p. 190.
33. ibid. p. 190.
34. H. L. Wilensky, *The Welfare State and Equality*, University of California Press 1975, pp. 22 ff.
35. OECD, *Public Expenditure Trends*, Paris 1978, Table 6, p. 25.
36. ibid. 'Welfare' as defined in this calculation excludes public provision for housing, the true welfare element in this field being especially hard to identify. It is possible that in consequence the relative welfare performance of countries, such as Britain, which have put a heavy emphasis on public housing provision is understated.
37. ibid. Table 12, p. 42.
38. Heidenheimer *et al.*, *Comparative Public Policy*, pp. 214–15.
39. H. Heclo, *Modern Social Politics in Britain and Sweden: From Relief to Income Maintenance*, Yale University Press 1974, p. 283.
40. See, for instance, his essay on 'Distributive Justice' in Peter Laslett and W. G. Runciman (eds.), *Philosophy, Politics and Society*, Basil Blackwell, Oxford 1967, and his *Theory of Justice*, Oxford University Press 1972, pp. 75 ff. and ch. V, 'Distributive Shares'.
41. This conclusion is clearly contentious and would have to take account of such developments as the 'Great Society' reforms in the United States which were aimed specifically at groups of people identified as suffering from extreme disadvantage. The argument is not that such elements in the social movement were completely absent, but that they tended often, like the organization of President Johnson's reforms, to be ephemeral or weak by comparison with the other movements referred to in the text.
42. The proportion was 3 and 3½ per cent respectively for Germany and Sweden, but rose to 11 per cent in Canada, 13 per cent in the USA, and 16 per cent in France. See OECD, *Public Expenditure on Income Maintenance Programmes* (1976), Table 29, p. 72, and p. 80. Chap-

ter 5, pp. 67–8, discusses the poverty-line concept and defines the criterion used here, the 'standardized relative poverty line', which is equivalent to a rough average of national poverty lines.

43. ibid. p. 80.
44. OECD, *Public Expenditure Trends,* p. 30.
45. For a general discussion of the nefarious effect of democratic pressures on the process of balancing the budget, see James M. Buchanan and Richard E. Wagner, *Democracy in Deficit – The Political Legacy of Lord Keynes,* Academic Press, London 1977, especially chs 8, 9, and 10.
46. See C. P. Kindleberger, *Europe's Post-War Growth – The Role of Labor Supply,* Harvard University Press 1967.
47. See *The Social Framework,* OUP, 4th edn 1971, pp. 229 f., where the chief factor in the performance of the high-growth countries is said to be that 'they have . . . been able to increase their manufacturing population (as well as the labour engaged in service trades) as a result of a massive movement of labour out of agriculture . . . In the manufacturing sector, much more capital was required to employ the extra labour; it could not have been employed in these new ways if there had not been the extra capital; but the availability of labour meant that new, and very productive opportunities for the investment of the capital were rather easily found.'
48. ibid. Table 5, p. 74.
49. CEC, *European Economy,* Brussels 1979, Special Issue, 'Changes in Industrial Structure in the European Economies since the Oil Crisis, 1973–78', p. 60. See Table V-1, p. 57, for changes in employment in 1970–3, when secondary industry was already shedding labour, though in a more modest way than subsequently.
50. For an American view of the importance of producer services, see Eli Ginzberg (Chairman, US National Committee for Manpower Policy), 'The Pluralistic Economy of the US', *Scientific American,* vol. 235, no. 6 (Dec. 1976), p. 28.
51. *Editorial note: Andrew Shonfield's working papers for this section included a number of notes for the modification of its contents which he did not have time to incorporate in the text. Some of these are appended below:*

Productivity in 1960s
    1. The direct contribution of manufacturing value-added per capita to high growth *is* exaggerated (Hicks falls into this error in his *obiter dicta:* the idea that high investment per capita means very high productivity growth). 'Traded services', which include transport and communications, have higher productivity (in the European Com-

munity). But not 'commerce' (see OECD, *Economic Outlook,* no. 25, July 1979, 'Sectorial Shifts and Productivity Growth', pp. 28–35).

2. There is confusion about *classification* – e.g. 'repairs' are a traded service; but maintenance of equipment done by manufacturers (for consumers) and in a factory is part of the manufacturing process.

See John Hicks's interesting comment in *The Social Framework,* p. 74, on the reclassification of motor mechanics working in garages out of manufacturing into services.

3. Classification of 'industry' is difficult. *Primary* products, like coal and oil, should be included; if so, the proportion, including fuel and power, represented by industrial activity rises to 37 per cent for European Community countries. Indications, from partial data (see CEC, *European Economy,* Brussels 1979, Special Issue, p. 92), are that adding transport and communications would raise the total above 40 per cent.

4. The important point is that *the growth of manufacturing industry was (in the 1960s), and is, the pace-setter for the economy.* (This is the kernel of truth in Nicholas Kaldor's extension of Verdoorn – see his lecture on the *Causes of the Slow Rate of Growth of the United Kingdom,* Cambridge University Press 1966.) A substantial part of services is ancillary to industry, e.g. growing expenditure on maintenance of increased stock of household equipment.

5. It is wrong to move to panic conclusions, as in OECD report by R. A. Jenness, *Manpower and Employment,* p. 39, that we require a continuation of 4.5 per cent annual increase in 'industrial productivity' to maintain real incomes, but the saturation of markets will not permit this without higher unemployment – therefore we must export more manufactures to non-OECD markets!

52. Between 1960 and 1973 the increase in the number of people in employment in Japan was nearly 8 million (18 per cent). This net growth concealed a decrease of over 6 million in the number employed in agriculture. The secondary and tertiary sectors divided more or less evenly the gross increase of a little over 14 million additional workers.

See OECD, *Manpower and Employment,* pp. 37–8.

Productivity growth rates for Japan, over the rather shorter period 1963–73, were as follows:

Government	0.9
Agriculture	7.3
Industries	8.9
(Manufacturing)	(9.4)

Commerce   7.7
Other activities   7.7
                          ─────
    Total economy   8.7

See OECD, *Economic Outlook,* no. 25, Table 11, p. 29.

53. See OECD, *Manpower and Employment.*
54. See OECD, *Interfutures* Report, p. 153. The periods compared are 1960–8 with 1969–75.
55. G. L. Perry, 'Determinants of Wage Inflation around the World', *Brookings Papers on Economic Activity,* No. 2, Washington 1975.
56. OECD, *Interfutures* Report, p. 123. See also the interesting analysis of the German experience in the Bundesbank *Monthly Report,* January 1980.

Notes to Chapter 2 (pp. 37-66)

1. *Editorial note: The author's notes contain an alternative formulation which is relevant here.*

   There are two main groups of accusers; their underlying theses and the assumptions about the working of the economy are quite different, though in political terms they often coalesce. It is worth distinguishing them, if only to be able to identify more readily the particular variations of the dominant themes – because these are many. One is the monetarist critique, associated most especially with Milton Friedman; this asserts that there is a 'natural rate' of unemployment for any given economy and that, when demand is pushed above the level by governments or central banks adding to the supply of money, the only effect (except in the very short term) is to increase not output, but prices. If governments keep on pushing in this way, then they buy their short-lived spurt in production at the cost of rising amounts of inflation. All the same, they can't do serious damage directly to the *real economy* by pumping in this extra money – though some harm could be caused if the additional money happened to be distributed in such a way as to cause a misallocation of resources at the margin. But if the economy is already at the rate of expansion that can be sustained without causing inflation (i.e. that corresponding to the 'natural rate'), it is only prices that respond to the further stimulus. Of course, if a succession of stimuli has created a large stock of extra money, then it will take that much more effort and time on the part of the authorities to put matters right. The required deflation of demand will, temporarily, reduce economic activity below the capacity to produce. But that is all. Nothing will have been damaged. With the monetary distortion removed, the economy operates at full capacity again, but without the distorting effect of inflation.

The other theory is that damage is more profound. [*The text breaks off here. A marginal note indicates that an exposition of Hayek's 'initially plausible' theories was to follow.*]

2. See Chapter 1, p. 31.
3. See, for the comparative data on employment and productivity, CEC, *European Economy*, Special Issue 1979, 'Changes in Industrial Structure in the European Economies since the Oil Crisis', ch. V.
4. See OECD, *Economic Outlook: Occasional Studies*, A. Mittelstädt, 'Unemployment Benefits and Related Payments in Seven Major Countries' (July 1975), Table 1. Tax concessions can on occasion make these short-term benefits more profitable than the fully taxed wages they replace. For a French example, see *Financial Times*, 22 Nov. 1978, p. 2.
5. W. A. Lewis, op. cit. p. 28.
6. ibid. p. 28.
7. See the table which follows:

Net financial deficit in government expenditure as a percentage of GNP

Countries	1973	1974	1975	1976	1977
United States	0.5	−0.2	− 4.2	2.1	−1.1
Germany	1.2	−1.4	5.8	−3.6	−2.7
France	0.9	0.6	− 2.2	−0.8	−1.2
United Kingdom	−2.5	−4.0	− 4.8	−4.9	−3.3
Italy	−6.3	−5.9	−14.5	−9.8	−9.9
Japan	−2.8*	−3.8*	−7.4*	−7.6*	−7.4*
Canada	1.0	1.8	− 2.3	−1.8	−2.7

* Includes public enterprises
Source: BIS, *Forty-Eighth Annual Report*, Basle (1977–8), p. 56.

8. See, for the detailed figures, OECD, *Economic Outlook*, Dec. 1976, no. 20, Tables 4 and 5, pp. 21, 24.
9. BIS, *Forty-Eighth Annual Report*, pp. 55 f.
10. See OECD, *Economic Outlook*, nos. 20 and 22, Table 5 in both, p. 24 and p. 21 respectively (note that the 1976 figure has been recalculated in the later table). The seven countries are the same as those listed in the BIS table above.
11. CEC, *Annual Report 1979–80*, p. 35.
12. ibid.

13. See, for typical, and influential, examples of the argument the Annual Reports of the German Council of Economic Experts (Sachverständigenrat), 1976 and 1977.

14. The European Council in April 1978, when agreement was reached on the need for a strategy to 'reverse the unsatisfactory trend in the Community's economic and social situation'.

15. The phrase used by the German Ministry of Finance in the official document explaining its change of course, *Der Finanzplan des Bundes, 1978–1982*, Drucksache 8/2151 (1978).

16. This is the sense of the argument developed in the 1978 Annual Report of the German Council of Economic Experts (Sachverständigenrat), Drucksache 8/2313, paras. 175, 307, 414–23. For the plan itself see *Der Finanzplan des Bundes, 1978–1982*.

17. See above, p. 44.

18. On this point see also the 1979 Annual Report of the German Council of Economic Experts (Sachverständigenrat), Drucksache 8/3420, para. 210.

19. For a more detailed account of the similarities, and differences, between the German *Finanzplan* and the French VIIIth Plan, 1981–5, see Andrew Shonfield's article in the *Revue Économique*, no. 5, Paris, Sept. 1980, pp. 826 ff.

20. Data from OECD, *Economic Survey of Germany*, May 1980.

21. The Snake comprised the following countries in the late 1970s: Germany, Belgium, Denmark, Netherlands, Norway, Sweden. The original 'Snake', as established in 1973, had also included France.

22. OECD, *Economic Outlook*, no. 25, July 1979, p. 19.

23. For a current statement of this view see K. Richebächer, *Im Teufelskreis der Wirtschaftspolitik*, Bonn Aktuell, Stuttgart 1980, especially pp. 259 ff. Richebächer argues that the German revival of 1979 was destined from the start to be a one-year wonder, which would have petered out in any case because of internal contradictions of demand management policy. The central bank, because of its concern with the increase of inflationary pressures in an economy with no margin of additional productive capacity, would have ensured that the fiscal stimulus to economic growth would have been cancelled out by the rise in interest rates. All that one can say is that in spite of higher interest rates, German industrial investment continued to advance in the first part of 1980. New productive capacity would have helped to meet higher levels of demand, and in the meanwhile the German government showed an unusual willingness to use its reserves and its borrowing capacity abroad to limit the inflationary effect of the boost to economic activity at home. What finally killed the boom was the

collapse of international trade in manufactures, on which the German economy is especially dependent, in the second half of 1980.

24. For a discussion of Hayek's present and former views, see his *New Studies in Philosophy, Politics, Economics and the History of Ideas*, Routledge, London 1978, pp. 206–7. John Hicks has shown how eccentric Hayek's analysis and proposed remedy was when it was made in the 1930s and how the adoption of his formula then would certainly have made a bad situation even worse (see 'The Hayek Story' in *Critical Essays in Monetary Theory*, Oxford 1967). Hicks goes on to an ingenious specification of how the conditions postulated by Hayek, leading to a slump characterized by high wages and too little saving to sustain investment, might occur (ibid. pp. 214 f.). However, a characteristic feature of the economic slowdown of the 1970s was a general rise in personal savings to an unusually high level and a failure of business investment to absorb them. Governments then stepped in to borrow the additional money on offer in order to finance increased budget deficits, which reflected the effort to fill the financial gap created by the fall in private business activity. It is possible that there may have been some 'crowding out' of business borrowing by governments in consequence, and in this sense some business investment that would otherwise have occurred could have been discouraged by a shortage of capital or by its high price. But this was certainly not a general phenomenon and, as shown above, most governments hurried to cut back their borrowing demands very sharply as soon as the first signs of any recovery of business demand appeared. Moreover, it is noteworthy that in the countries where governments did not cut back, notably in Japan and the United States, business investment went ahead more vigorously than elsewhere.

25. Services have a weight of one third in the consumer price index and public services are one-twelfth. See OECD Economic Surveys of Japan, 1977 and 1979, for statistics cited here and in the following text.

26. Much of this expenditure, on capital projects, does not appear in the regular budget. It is financed directly by public borrowing which goes to the Fiscal Investment and Loan Plan (FILP), an organization with vast resources which is responsible for long-term investment in which the public authorities have an interest. Its activities increased so massively during the period of the economic slowdown of the second half of the 1970s that the payment of interest on the money that it had borrowed from the public came to be a serious burden on the regular budget. For further data on the FILP operation in the middle and late 1970s see ibid., Table 12 (1977) and Table 13 (1979).

27. Samuel Brittan and P. Lilley, *The Delusion of Incomes Policy,* Temple Smith, London 1977, Preface, p. 7. The book is deliberately polemical in tone, but well expresses the underlying spirit of the monetarist critique of attempts to interfere with the process of market determination of prices, whether in labour or commodity markets. Japan is, incidentally, not one of the countries whose experience is included in the survey.

28. The careful and detailed survey of American experience, C. D. Goodwin (ed.), *Exhortation and Controls: The Search for a Wage–Price Policy, 1945–1970* (Brookings, Washington 1975), is particularly valuable as a study of a variety of administrative methods and of the appropriate criteria of analysis to be applied to the results.

29. OECD, *Incomes and Employment Policies Related to Medium-Term Growth,* International Seminar Series 1977/2⁰, Paris (April 1978).

30. G. L. Perry, 'Stabilization policy and inflation' in H. Owen and C. L. Schultze (eds.), *Setting National Priorities: The Next Ten Years,* Brookings, Washington 1976, p. 306.

31. ibid. p. 310.

32. Hayek is in this matter, too, led to a confident, and highly dubious, conclusion about the perverse consequences of modern economic planning, by insisting on an archaic image of what a plan is about – a composite, in his view, of rigid expectations which must, predictably, fail; see his essay, 'The New Confusion About "Planning" ', in *The Morgan Guarantee Survey,* New York (Jan. 1976).

33. A. M. Okun, 'Inflation: its Mechanics and Welfare Costs', in A. M. Okun and G. L. Perry (eds.), *Brookings Papers on Economic Activity* (1975: 2), p. 365. Much of the argument here derives from this article, which provides a succinct summary of Okun's extensive work on this subject.

34. ibid., Editors' Summary, p. 252.

35. ibid., Editors' Summary, p. 252. See also the argument developed at greater length in Okun's earlier work, 'Upward Mobility in High-pressure Economy', in *Brookings Papers on Economic Activity* (1973: 1), pp. 235–44.

36. The argument outlined above about 'customer' as against 'auction' markets bears a close relationship to John Hicks's distinction between 'fixprice' and 'flexprice' products. See *The Crisis in Keynesian Economics,* Blackwell, Oxford 1974, especially pp. 29 f. and 77 ff., for a telling analysis of the adverse consequences for policy-making of ignoring this key difference in market behaviour.

Notes to Chapter 3 (pp. 67-93)

1. For an account of the nature of the business cycle in the two decades which followed the end of the Second World War see the author's *Modern Capitalism*, Oxford University Press 1965, pp. 11 ff.
2. *Interfutures*, p. 162. The data on which this claim is founded are summarized in the following table (ibid. p. 163), which divides the period from 1960 to the middle 1970s into three five-year sequences:

Boom year unemployment rates in some OECD countries

	1960/65		*1966/70*		*1971/76*	
USA			(1966)	3.6	(1973)	4.7
Canada			(1966)	3.5	(1973)	5.6
France	(1964)	1.1	(1969	1.6	(1973)	2.0
Germany	(1965)	0.5	(1970)	0.6	(1973)	1.0
Italy	(1962)	2.9	(1970)	3.1	(1973)	3.4
United Kingdom	(1964)	1.4			(1973)	2.3
Netherlands	(1965)	0.8	(1969)	1.4	(1973)	2.4
Belgium	(1965)	1.7	(1970)	1.8	(1973)	2.2
Sweden	(1964)	1.6	(1970)	1.5	(1974)	2.0

Source: OECD employment statistics

3. OECD, *Economic Outlook*, no. 27 (July 1980), Historical Statistics, p. 143. Aggregate figures are weighted in terms of the relative private consumption of component countries. Accordingly, the trend in the US is the major influence on the outcome.
4. ibid. The weighted average of the annual percentage increase in consumer prices during the years immediately preceding the great inflation was as follows:

	1968	*1969*	*1970*	*1971*	*1972*
Seven major OECD countries	4.1	5.0	5.6	5.0	4.4
Total OECD	4.0	4.8	5.6	5.3	4.8

5. ibid.
6. See OECD, *Economic Outlook*, no. 18 (Dec. 1975), pp. 24–7 and pp. 44 f., for a discussion of this phenomenon.
7. For Paul Volcker's (chairman, FRB) action on 14 March 1980 to curb inflationary pressures, see *Financial Times*, 17 March 1980, pp. 13–14. The programme included guidelines, both qualitative and quantitative, on bank credit and measures to increase the cost of some forms of lending, including credit cards. Further measures to curb consumer spending were taken by the FRB in the summer of 1980.

8. OECD, *Economic Outlook*, no. 27, p. 40.
9. The earliest concerted initiative aimed at reducing the shock was presented at an IMF meeting of the 'Committee of Twenty' on 18–19 January 1974 by the Fund's Managing Director Dr Johannes Witeveen. It established a 'temporary supplementary facility' within the IMF, under which resources would be made available to assist members – in particular developing countries – in meeting the impact of the increased oil prices on their balances of payment. The special funds for financing this facility were made available to the IMF by loans from oil-producing countries. The support granted by this scheme was extended from one year to three years by a decision in mid-September 1974.

     Later that month Denis Healey, then UK Chancellor of the Exchequer, proposed a parallel facility within the IMF for industrialized countries. The theme of a strategy for developing and industrialized countries alike was taken up and elaborated by the US Secretary of State, Henry Kissinger, a month later in a speech delivered on 14 November 1974.

     It was an earlier initiative of Kissinger's that had laid down the groundwork for a new co-ordinating institution, the International Energy Agency. The IEA was formed under the umbrella of the OECD in November 1974, and comprises twenty-one member-countries (France being a notable exception).
10. Professor Bela Balassa has shown by means of an approximate calculation the effect of a more expansionary domestic policy – with a rate of economic growth such as France achieved between 1973 and 1978 (2.9 per cent), instead of the German actual rate of 1.7 per cent – on German import demand. Germany would in such circumstances have faced in 1978 a trade deficit of the order of 5 billion dollars instead of an actual surplus of 25 billion dollars. See his 'L'économie française sous la cinquième république, 1958–1978', *Révue Economique*, no. 6 (Nov. 1979), Paris.
11. See OECD, *Economic Outlook*, no. 27, Table 33, p. 118. The average rise in the index of energy prices, weighted on the basis of the energy demand of the seven largest OECD countries, was 113 (1972 = 100).
12. This calculation is based on the United Nations Index of Export Prices of Manufactures, quoted in NIESR, *Economic Review*, London, Nov. 1979, Table 3, p. 40.
13. This is the title of the book edited by F. Hirsch and J. H. Goldthorpe (Robinson, London 1978) in which Brittan's essay 'Inflation and Democracy' appeared. See p. 185 for the passage quoted.

14. The communiqué of the Summit Conference in July 1979 of the leaders of the seven major Western economies – USA, Japan, Germany, Britain, France, Italy, and Canada – clearly expresses the spirit of the changed approach to international economic policy. Perhaps its most striking feature is the absence of any reference to a need for some measure of co-ordination, which would avoid a merely competitive national approach to the balance of payments problem caused by the oil price rise, despite the fact that a large aggregate deficit was inevitably going to be incurred by the rest of the world with the oil-exporting countries.

15. See GATT, *International Trade 1978/79*, Geneva 1979, p. 5. The percentage share of intra-OECD trade in total world commerce fell by 6 per cent between 1973 and 1978, wiping out in these five years the whole of the gain which it had secured during the ten years of expansion preceding 1973.

16. By that time the servicing of Poland's debts to Western lending institutions absorbed well over two-thirds of the country's foreign exchange earnings in Western markets. This imposed a burden on its balance of payments which severely limited the Polish government's room for manoeuvre in coping with the political crisis of the early 1980s by means of further concessions to consumer demands.

17. Interestingly, West Germany, which had been the outstanding practitioner of exclusively national political economy in the early 1970s, was notable in the second business cycle as the country which showed some sensitiveness to the international repercussions of a too vigorous pursuit of domestic policies aimed at the restoration of balance of payments equilibrium. Chancellor Helmut Schmidt in 1980 issued warnings about this; however, the Bundesbank, showing its familiar independence, continued to give the traditional German priority to the balance of payments objective.

18. It was a boom of major proportions which put an extra 12 million Americans into employment. The extent of US domestic inflation was given a dramatic character by the somewhat exaggerated figure (13 per cent) registered by the official Consumer Price Index (CPI) in 1979, partly caused by the peculiar construction of that index with its heavy weighting of interest rate changes. The alternative measure, the 'deflator' used to identify the price movements which did not affect the real national product, showed a rise of under 10 per cent. Taking a somewhat longer view and concentrating on those changes that were induced by domestic developments rather than external events, Charles Schultze, Chairman of the Council of Economic Advisers, calculated that between 1977 and 1979 the annual rise in these

prices had gone up from 6 per cent to 8 per cent; see his speech of 22 February 1980 to an audience in Miami, Florida.

19. C. P. Kindleberger, *The World in Depression, 1929–1939*, Allen Lane, London 1973, pp. 297–308 *passim*.
20. See OECD, *Interfutures*, p. 167, citing data from D. H. Freedman, 'Employment Perspectives in Industrialized Market Economy Countries', *International Labour Review*, vol. 117, no. 1 (Jan.–Feb. 1978), p. 16.
21. OECD, *A Medium-Term Strategy for Employment and Manpower Policies* (1978), p. 19. The actual figures were within the range of 15–18 per cent of total job opportunities in different countries, with a ten-year growth rate of five percentage points – three-quarters of these part-time jobs being filled by women.
22. This is a view which pervades the thinking of Jonathan Gershuny; see, for example, his and R. E. Pahl's article, 'Britain in the decade of the three economies', *New Society* (3 Jan. 1980), London.
23. See, for instance, the proposals of Arthur Burns, then Chairman of the US Federal Reserve Board, in 'The Real Issues of Inflation and Unemployment', a lecture at the University of Georgia (1975).
24. *Monthly Report of the German Bundesbank*, January 1980, 'The Growth of Productivity in the Federal Republic of Germany and its Determinants', p. 13. Other data in the text on German productivity trends are also derived from this source.
25. ibid.
26. This is a factor making for the more rapid rise in productivity in Europe and Japan than in the United States over the post-war period, which is particularly stressed by A. Maddison, op. cit. As he observes, the United States was providing a species of free international public good, in the form of technical innovation, to the rest of the industrial world.
27. The same has been true of Japan.
28. For a clear statement of the political consequences of this theory see B. T. McCallum, 'The Significance of Rational Expectation Theory', *Challenge* (Jan.–Feb. 1980).
29. See A. Lindbeck, 'Stabilization Policy in Open Economies with Endogenous Politicians', Richard T. Ely Lecture, *American Economic Review*, vol. 66, no. 2, May 1976, for an especially telling analysis of the way in which selective and discriminatory intervention by governments (which Lindbeck regards as necessary for the management of the contemporary business cycle) tends to be severely limited by the accidents of electoral timing. Note that this is a quite different problem from that faced by governments which embark on new poli-

cies that can only be expected to show their results properly in the medium term – typically the position of governments like that of Mrs Thatcher in Britain and Monsieur Barre in France during the late 1970s – and which require the indulgence of the electorate for more than one political cycle. The latter is a familiar and long-standing problem of conducting long-term innovative policies in a democracy.
30. OECD, Paris (1975). The author, Niels Thygesen, bases his results on a review of the experience of six countries – USA, UK, France, Italy, Germany, and Japan – from 1960 to 1972.

Notes to The Argument Continued (pp. 98-115)

1. See for example OECD, *Public Expenditure on Income Maintenance*, Paris 1976.
2. See E. C. Ladd Jr. and S. M. Lipset, 'Anatomy of a Decade', *Dialogue*, no. 50 (4/1980), p. 3.
3. For a fuller comparison of French and German economic policies see the author's 'The VIIIth Plan; Assumptions and Constraints', *Revue Économique*, vol. 31, no. 5 (Sept. 1980), Paris, pp. 826–36.
4. Such as the authors (B. M. Blechman, E. M. Gramlich, and R. W. Hartman) of the Brookings Institution study, *Setting National Priorities – The 1975 Budget*, Washington 1974. The quotation below is on p. 247.
5. Andrew Shonfield, 'The Politics of the Mixed Economy in the International System of the 1970s', *International Affairs*, vol. 56, no. 1 (Jan. 1980), London, p. 5.
6. Lester C. Thurow, *The Zero-Sum Society – Distribution and the Possibilities for Economic Change*, New York 1980.
7. This essay originally appeared in 1929 as the Rhodes Memorial Lectures and was published in 1930 by the Clarendon Press, Oxford. It has been republished in a collection of Halévy's essays, *The Era of Tyrannies*, by Anchor Books, Doubleday, New York 1965.

Index